Praise for *The Poetics of Sales*

"I used say that I would never want to be a salesperson. Only in recent years have I come to understand that everyone with an inspired message must be a salesperson to have his voice heard. It is with this growing realization that I embrace Mr. Lansford's convicting advice to build transformational relationships that endure the test of time and competition. I'm convinced that Mr. Lansford's eighteen codes resonate in any sales context for salespersons of all stripes."

Dr. Harold L. Arnold, Jr.
Author of *Second Shift: How to Grow Your Part-Time Passion to Full-Time Influence*.
Marriage ROCKS for Christian Couples.

"*The Poetics of Sales* is a masterpiece of insightful and successful experience that pinpoints the *true* heart of the matter in regards to successful sales. A must-read for sales people at all levels, this book is golden, and one that I will use and implement in my organization as well as my professional career. No matter what level of experience one has, this book will refocus and sharpen all who are in a sales profession!"

Jeff Strametz
President / CEO
Boulder Creek Musical Instrument

"Ernie is a testimony to 'Work Smart' and 'Practice What You Teach.' He writes from real-life experience, backed up by years of personal and professional success. He's an honest, gentle man who has fostered success for many and continues to learn and help others succeed. Ernie learned that success comes from helping others, whether it be family, friends, your company, or customers. Here he shared how he did it."

Donald Mitchell
Retired EVP Sales
MIDCO International

"Ernie's many years of professional sales experience have proven the simple truth that if you maintain a focus on developing strong, mutually beneficial relationships and *genuinely* care about your customers, good things will happen. This requires diligence, integrity, and discipline; there are no shortcuts, tricks, or techniques. However, there definitely is a *right* way to approach sales. The concepts covered in *The Poetics of Sales* are foundational to sustainable success in business . . . and in life."

Jeff Radke
Executive Vice President-Sales
Sweetwater Sound

"While I knew Ernie Lansford from his stellar reputation in the music products industry, my first opportunity to work with him directly came in the late 1990s when I was Chairman of the Board at the International Music Products Association, or NAMM. One of our challenges was that we were often misunderstood and viewed by our constituents as "government." Because of this, the valuable member benefits we provided often went unappreciated and underutilized. Ernie was brought on as a Director of Business Development charged with reaching out to our commercial members to improve awareness and utilization of NAMM services. The relationships Ernie helped us build brought countless members closer to the Association and continue to pay dividends almost two decades later. These lingering, long-lasting results are the true measure of Ernie's effectiveness."

Gerson Rosenbloom,
VP of Strategic Management, Sweetwater Sound
Former Chairman of the Board, NAMM

"As fast as the world is changing, much of business culture is still stuck in models that were conceived in the late '50s. We all tell ourselves to be agile, flexible, and open to change, but often we are only willing to make small incremental changes to the habits of the past. Ernie Lansford is unusual in that he actually works at staying mentally agile. He is intensely curious, extremely generous, and doesn't put himself above his customers, employees, and coworkers.

His philosophy of service is deeply ingrained in me—it's a philosophy that can seem paradoxical at times, in the sense that the best results come from being of the greatest service. The idea that you get what you need when you are the least selfish. Ernie isn't a man of buzzwords, he is a man of thought and action."

John Anning
National Sales Manager
Piano Dealer Channel—Casio EMI

"I believe it is nearly impossible for anyone to teach that which they have not done, at least not credibly. On the complete opposite end of the spectrum, having Ernie Lansford share his life's lessons on sales and customer service is a great gift to us all. When I worked in music retail, Ernie would visit our store and energize us with his passion for self-improvement, letting us know in no uncertain terms that selling was indeed a noble calling. Throughout his career, Ernie worked with many of the giants of our industry and studied the classic teachings of the selling masters. He shares with us now his unique interpretations of these lessons and distills them down to 18 tested and proven Immutable Codes. With this book, I imagine his positive influence will be felt for years and years to come."

Joe Lamond
CEO/President NAMM (International Music Products Assn)

"When you're deep in the hole and you can only see the rim you just tumbled over and into the dark, Ernie is the guy who without hesitation will jump right in there with you. And when you exclaim, 'Great! Now both of us are stuck in here!' Ernie kindly reveals, 'That's right, and it's okay. I've been here before, and I know the way out . . . now let's go!'

Here are Ernie's 18 Immutable Codes (ways) to get yourself out of that sales hole and become a celebrated Customer Success Master. You'll quickly discover as I did, these Codes are relevant to much more than sales success. He's given us a great blueprint for living life and serving others."

Don Young
Founder/Managing Director
Agile Partners

The Poetics of Sales

A Sales Rep's Journey from Tolerated Professional Visitor to Celebrated Partner

Ernie Lansford

The Poetics of Sales
© Business Development Concepts, LLC

All right reserved. No portion of this book may be reproduced, stored in a retrieval system, or transmitted in any form or by any means—electronic, mechanical, photocopy, recording or any other—without the prior written permission of the publisher, except for brief quotations in printed reviews.

Published in Indian Harbour Beach, FL by
Business Development Concepts, LLC.
274 Eau Gallie Blvd. Ste 310
Indian Harbour Beach, FL 32937
(615) 656 - 5330

Business Development Concepts, LLC titles and on-site seminars may be purchased for educational, business, fundraising, or sales promotional use. For information, please email
ernie@ernielansford.coach

Unless otherwise indicated, Scripture quotations are taken from the New King James Version (NKJV), Copyright 1979, 1980, 1982, 1992, 2005, by Thomas Nelson, Inc. Used by permission. All rights reserved.
Scripture quotations marked MSG are taken from The Message Copyright © 1993, 1994, 1995, 1996, 2000, 2001, 2002 by Eugene H. Peterson

Edited by Jennifer Harshman
Cover design by E. Clark emilyclark.no.e@gmail.com
Printed in the United States of America

Author's Note

I am a person of faith. I do my best to share my faith in my deeds, actions and relationships rather than words. Although occasionally I use Old and NewTestament Scripture for illustration and to support my position, this book isn't an evangelistic type book. I desire for you to understand the difference between the traditional account manager/sales rep focused on transactions and Customer Success Mastery© focused on relationship centric activities by treating customers as you desire to be treated.

This passage from Psalms 61:5–8 is the foundation for my purpose in writing the book.

"You've always taken me seriously, God,

made me welcome among those who know and love you.

Let the days of the king add up

to years and years of good rule.

Set his throne in full light of God;

post Steady Love and Good Faith as lookouts,

And I'll be the poet who sings your glory--

and live what I sing every day."

The Message (MSG)

Editor's Note

Poetics of Sales came to me through Nick Pavlidis, because I edit everything written by authors he coaches, by Nick and the people at his agency. Ernie didn't hire me, and it's possible he didn't even know of me. As I edited this book, I nodded and said, "Yes!" throughout. Good business is all about taking excellent care of people. We've all seen it done wrong. This book shows how to do it right. Ernie Lansford earned a Celebrated Relationship with me through his words—probably before he even knew my name. I am now blessed by his friendship, and I hope you are blessed by his words and make great use of them.

Jennifer Harshman
Writing and Publishing Expert

Dedication

I dedicate this labor of love to Jennifer Lansford, my wife of 51 years (as of March 2019), and my children, Ernie Lansford III, and Christie Lansford Waechter.

Their sacrifice and understanding of my drive to succeed as a sales representative and eventually senior leadership in corporate America cannot be expressed in words. I found a quote by Reverend Billy Graham that is essential to this book.

Dr. Graham was asked how he could have had a greater impact in the world. Grahams response shook me. "I've spoken to stadiums packed with 80,000 and 90,000 people," he responded. "But if I would have spent more time with my children, I would have had a greater impact on the world."

Dr. Graham's quote reminded me to not let my career, ambitions and wanting to get "bigger" be nearly as important as my family

Looking back over 51+ years of marriage and parenting, I now realize I was selfish. I should have taken Dr. Graham's advice sooner. Long trips away from home, sometimes for several weeks out of the country were not necessary. I love and thank them deeply for allowing me to have an affair with my career. Fortunately, I still have my family in spite of my perceived failure as a husband and dad.

Please, take my advice. ***<u>Do as I say, not as I did</u>***. Build Celebrated Relationships with your family first and foremost to enjoy a truly successful life.

Special Acknowledgement

This book has been a work in progress since I was a child. You will learn more about my "why" later in the book, where I explain Immutable Customer Success Code #9 on Commitment and Perseverance. I have wanted to write a book about the art of Customer Success Mastery© for as long as I can remember. I started the process in the 1970s with scribbled notes in a Nifty brand spiral bound notebook like I used in high school. I had notes to myself everywhere. When the digital age came upon us, I created folders in Outlook, Apple Mail, and eventually Google Drive. All those notes are worthless without action. A goal without a plan of action is a dream, which could become a nightmare if we do not create a plan of action to achieve the goals.

Nick Pavlidis was my catalyst to make this book happen. Nick was my writing coach, confidant, mentor, and friend. Without Nick's input, wordsmith skills, and generosity to make this book happen it would still be a disorganized manuscript in a digital file folder on G-Drive. Nick guided me in condensing my original 250 page manuscript to 132 pages to clarify my message. I cannot express in mere words my gratitude and heartfelt thanks to Nick for making *Poetics of Sales* a reality. I added his name on the cover as a simple symbol of appreciation for his coaching.

I recommend Nick as a writing coach (he's an awesome legal counsel, too). All of us have a book inside that needs to be printed physically or digitally. Contact Nick at nick@nickpavlidis.com

Acknowledgements

I am a curator of ideas I gained through 53+ years of sales leadership. Frankly, I have lost track of my original vs. inspired ideas. Ed Phipps, George Prewitt, Earl Nightingale, Napoleon Hill, Norman Vincent Peal, Zig Ziglar, Hank Trisler, Tom Hopkins, Joe Lamond, John C. Maxwell, Michael Hyatt, Dan Miller, Fay Adkins, Dale Carnegie, Hartley Peavey, Eugene Kornblum, Don Mitchell, Larry Linkin, Melia Peavey, August Turak, Mark Altekruse, William Hatcher, Gerson Rosenbloom, Aaron Walker, Bob Beaudine, Ken Fuente, George Hines, Skip Maggiora, Bob Bankston, Christie and Eric Waechter, Ernie Lansford, III, Dave Ramsey, Alex Nelson, Royce White, Mike Lansford, Sr., my parents Ernest and Eva Lansford, and many others are a few of my influencers!

DISCLAIMER: Sales concepts, ideas and strategies shared within are ideas that have worked for me, members of my various teams, students, clients, and friends. They are not specific advice for your business. Always use your own judgment and/or get the advice of professionals to find the right strategies for your business and your particular situation. I want to help you change people's lives by creating Celebrated Relationships. I want to help you grow a real business that supports your dreams by helping you elevate your sales career to the next level. I want you to be part of future incredible materials that will change your business and your life. And I don't want you to miss out on any of it.

Website: ~~www.ernielansford~~

Email: *Ernie@ernielansford.coach*

Table of Contents

Preface……………………………………………..…..1
Foreword………………………..……………..…....…7
Introduction……………………………………..……11
Immutable Customer Success Code #1………….31
Immutable Customer Success Code #2………....37
Immutable Customer Success Code #3………....41
Immutable Customer Success Code #4………....47
Immutable Customer Success Code #5………....53
Immutable Customer Success Code #6….……...57
Immutable Customer Success Code #7….……...61
Immutable Customer Success Code #8………....63
Immutable Customer Success Code #9…..……..69
Immutable Customer Success Code #10………..79
Immutable Customer Success Code #11………..87
Immutable Customer Success Code #12………..91
Immutable Customer Success Code #13………..97
Immutable Customer Success Code #14……...101
Immutable Customer Success Code #15……...105
Immutable Customer Success Code #16……...111
Immutable Customer Success Code #17……...115
Immutable Customer Success Code #18……...121
Your Next Step…………………………………...125

Preface

I hope my experience, success and failures I share in this book will help you increase sales, margins, and profits. In my opinion you will go higher in your sales career if you subscribe to the ideas and concepts within and work to earn what I call *Celebrated Relationships* with your customers. If you do that, you'll have achieved a status most salespeople never do, a *Customer Success Master*®.

A poem called "One Man Awake," by Helen Kromer, succinctly captures exactly what happens when Customer Success Masters operate with a passion for service to their customers and earn Celebrated Relationship status. In the poem, Ms. Kromer described one man awakening another, the second awakening his neighbor, the three rousing the town, and so forth until so many people are awake that everyone is awakened by the fuss. The message in the poem is in Ms. Kromer's conclusion, that when one man wakes up with passion, the passion multiplies. I want your passion about your business, your life, and your customers, to multiply like Ms. Kromer describes in "One Man Awake." This book is designed to help you do just that.

Who influences you?
Like many of you, there have been and continue to be many people who have influenced me in my personal and professional life. Some influences were not good, some were mediocre, and others were great. This book is a small accumulation or accounting of the wisdom I learned from the great influencers in and on my personal and professional life.

Frankly, the influencers were so impactful on me that I have lost sight of which of the Codes are original to my observations, borrowed, or stolen, so to speak, from those amazing people (big grin here). That's the beauty of wisdom. It builds on itself and transcends time. As you read this, you'll see that I give attribution when I remember someone else as being the source of the content within. At the end, however, these lessons are not about me or them. They are about you and your future customers. Take these lessons and implement them into your business and personal life, like I have done over the past five decades, and you'll build deep relationships that can serve you, your family, your customers, and even your customers' customers.

These Codes impact all of your relationships.
Everyone we meet is a current customer or probable customer. Some are internal some are external. Some are direct some are indirect. Regardless of the type of customer everyone we meet is a customer and everyone we meet is a sales professional too. We have a responsibility to add value and significance to guide each other on our life journey.

All of us are both salespeople and customers. We sell and buy all day long. Whether it's an idea, product, or service, we're all buying and selling all day long. I have a strong desire to help those who are called and/or following their true passion, or their why, in a professional setting as compensated sales professionals who understand the importance of adding significance to their customers and their customers. These Codes will help you do that.

There are five levels of the salesperson-customer relationship.

Over the years, I've defined five levels of a relationship: Tolerated, Acknowledged, Vendor, Partner, and Celebrated. Unfortunately, most of the world views compensated sales professionals as Tolerated, Acknowledged, or Vendor at best. Partner level is far better than the lower three levels, but not easily attained. If you find yourself in one of three lower levels, your fulfillment and earnings will be limited compared to those salespeople who develop Partner and Celebrated Relationships with their customers. There are very few true Partner level relationships and Celebrated Relationships in business is rare. Most of us reserve Celebrated Relationship status for our loved ones and then only a select few of our loved ones such as our spouse, children, or parents are worthy of a celebrated status. Yet there's no reason you can't build Celebrated Relationships with your best customers. These Codes will help you do that.

In Google, searching "to celebrate" tells us it means to acknowledge a significant or happy day or event with a gathering or enjoyable activity. We can do that in business by helping our customers help their customers. When our customer's customers thrive and prosper by finding transformative values of our products and services, our customers celebrate. They celebrate deeper relationships with their customers. They celebrate success in their business. And they celebrate the salesperson (you) who helped them serve their customers well.

In fact, every completed transaction is a celebration of a commitment to the value we see in each other. Every completed transaction is a celebration of our commitment to the relationship to help each other thrive, prosper, and grow.

If you add enough value for your customers, the celebration will continue and grow deeper over time. According to best-selling author and leadership expert, John C. Maxwell, there are four ways to add value to others:

- Value others.
- Make yourself more valuable by growing and becoming better at what you do.
- Know and relate to what they value. Connect with them.
- Value what God values.

Dr. Maxwell's four ways of adding value to people are the basis for why I do what I do, or my *why* or *calling*, which is to help sales leaders like you become transformational or celebrated vs. transactional with your customers. I want to see you develop Celebrated Relationships with your customers, to have a long, fulfilled business and personal life.

What Dr. Maxwell describes as transformational leadership, I call Customer Success Mastery. It's the same principles applied to the concept of serving others through sales. Customer Success Mastery is the art of guiding others (customers) effectively to where they desire to go faster than they would get there alone. Complex on the surface, yet simple when you think about it and adopt a steward-leadership mindset.

We're all Customer Success Masters with a deep passion to serve others, our customers. Are you the one who needs to be awakened, or the one who is helping wake everyone else up? Are you the one with passion in your eyes or one whose eyes are blinded and unable to even see the noonday sun because you are focused on transactions rather than connecting and building relationships by adding significance to others?

Every great business starts with a transformational leader who had a dream of adding significance to the world and starts telling (or, in this case selling) others about it. Whether Martin Luther King or Martin Luther, they both had a vision and were willing to pay the price to speak it boldly. Whether Steve Jobs or Bill Gates, they both believed so strongly in what they created, that there was no one on Earth who could sway them. They all spoke and wrote about adding huge significance to the world.

Are you totally committed to the Customer Success Mastery of adding significance, or are you just along for the ride, gathering as many transactions as possible to build your own success?

Is your heart truly focused on adding significance to others by way of serving through your products or services, or only the outer you that everyone sees?

Please accept my words in this book as a small demonstration of my desire to see those of us practicing the art of selling be transformed from just Tolerated in the minds of our customers to forming Celebrated Relationships with them that will change the world.

As your life journey takes you to higher levels strive to be extraordinary in service to others, focused on the needs of others, confident in your actions and thankful for the opportunity to S.O.A.R.R.™ (Serving Others thru Actions & Relationships, Repeatedly). *Customer Success is The Mission; Celebrated Relationship is The Goal.*™

Thank you for reading this book.

Foreword

In the mid-1980s, I was a product manager for a well-established electronic music company based in Southern California. One of the duties of my job, and one that I truly enjoyed, was traveling to musical-instrument retailers all over the country. During these travels, I would train retail sales personnel on the finer selling points of the brand and the products and, very often, I was asked to help boost sell-through by conducting seminars and clinics for their customers.

It was during these travels when I first began to hear the name, Ernie Lansford. When discussing business with retailers, his name was often mentioned. Most of the time, retailers would express a fervent wish that all sales reps from all their suppliers were more like him. That's because he always solved problems. He always had words of encouragement for every one of his customers and for every person who worked for that customer.

It wasn't long before we were introduced to each other. For a number of years, I would see him occasionally at retailers, and we would also bump into each other at trade shows.

In late 2013, I was offered the opportunity to work with Ernie at a pro audio company located in the Pacific Northwest. In terms of corporate hierarchy, I reported to Ernie, yet, out of the gate, he treated me more as an equal rather than a subordinate. For several highly productive years, we worked together creating programs for our customers, helping each other over hurdles (him helping me more times than I can remember).

It was during this time that I first witnessed Ernie's passion for customer success. Ernie considered me a customer, too. He took responsibility for my mistakes and failures and gave me credit for my successes and wins. In his office, he had a huge dry-erase board where he would sketch ideas and concepts for building greater alliances with customers. We would talk for hours about those ideas and, eventually, we began to put some of those ideas into practice by producing a weekly video for the sales force, introducing them to ideas to promote customer success. The Tuesday Report was well received by our sales team. Ernie viewed them as customers, too. He believes in servant leadership with his team.

Many years before I met Ernie, I studied music performance, composition, and arranging at Berklee College of Music in Boston and later tackled deep instrument studies at the Musicians Institute (then known as the Guitar Institute of Technology) in Los Angeles. While attending GIT, one of the instructors, the late Bryant "Mac" McKernan, held regular classes on the major composers of the 20th Century. During my time at GIT, "Mac" and I became good friends and we spent countless hours listening to the music of these giants, and we had many late-into-the-night talks about these composers. At one point, "Mac" introduced me to *The Poetics of Music in the Form of Six Lessons*, a book authored by the late 20th Century composer, Igor Stravinsky. This book is from a series of lectures given by Stravinsky himself at the [Charles Eliot Norton Lecture Series at Harvard University](#) from 1939 to 1940.

One quote from this book, in particular, has resonated with me all these years:

"My freedom will be so much the greater and more meaningful the more narrowly I limit my field of action and the more I surround myself with obstacles. Whatever diminishes constraint diminishes strength. The more constraints one imposes, the more one frees one's self of the chains that shackle the spirit."

I remember reading this quote to Ernie during one of our lengthy, and frequent, video conference conversations. When first hearing or reading the quote, it seems as if it is coming out of left field. How can anyone obtain freedom if they are surrounded by obstacles? But after further thought and analysis, I learned that Stravinsky's deeper meaning is that his methodology is applicable to many endeavors. Allow me to explain.

The quote is referring to the complexities of composing for the symphony orchestra. Specifically, the daunting tasks and the fear one experiences when surrounded by the endless possibilities—the instrument groups, the varied combination of those groups, the ranges of pitch, timbre, dynamics, and so much more. With all that before you, how do you begin? Furthermore, what are you trying to communicate?

Ernie Lansford wrote this book based on his 53-plus years in the world of sales in the music products industry. It is a culmination of perspectives that he amassed from all his years working for companies and hundreds of coworkers and thousands of customers—many of whom have become lifelong friends of Ernie's.

One such perspective is the parallel which is the fundamental trait of Stravinsky's quote: you have to break down a problem into its essential elements and then combine the best of those elements to achieve a goal surrounded by obstacles.

In music, that goal is to create something that communicates and moves the audience. In the business of sales, the goal is to create a paradigm where people—your customers—will thrive and prosper. And while that prosperity could be the result of a product, a promotion, or a program, the most important trait of all sales leaders is knowing that continued prosperity is built on lasting relationships. Deep relationships with customers provide limitless opportunities when there is a foundation of mutual respect and trust.

Just as the composer uses the orchestra to navigate many obstacles to build emotion and lasting memories in the minds of the audience members, so does the sales leader in building trusted relationships. The sales leader's orchestra is made of people who each have specific goals and personalities. And just as the composer understands the abilities of every member of the orchestra and the limits of their instruments, so do successful sales leaders, because they understand the personalities of their customers, they know their customer's business models and their customer's end users. By breaking through the complexities of these relationships and understanding them, sales leaders create their own memorable "phrases" for their customers. Ultimately these creations provide opportunities for everyone to prosper.

The hallmark of a great composer is their ability to evoke emotions and create memories: the very foundation of a musical relationship. The hallmark of a great sales leader is in the quality of relationships and multitude of successes produced.

Ernie Lansford is a master in the world of Celebrated Relationships. This book is a testament to that fact.

Mark Altekruse
Sales and Development Professional

Discovering the Customer Success Codes and Customer Success Mastery

Customer Success Masters do not worry about job security or earning limits. Their customers are loyal customers who value and respect them. They don't need to cold call or chase purchase orders. They don't worry at the end of the month, quarter, or year. And they perform, year after year, in good markets and bad. They're the best of the best.

But most salespeople never achieve that level of success. Most salespeople have a few loyal customers but spend most of their time chasing purchase orders; traveling around the town, state, country, or world; working booths; doing demos; and pitching potential clients; only to see their competitors get the business.

The problem is most salespeople are trained to be transactional. Most salespeople are trained to constantly search for leads and establish relationships that are just deep enough to get a purchase order and move on. Because of that, they end up with shallow relationships and countless one-off sales transactions.

It doesn't have to be that way.

Top salespeople go far deeper than the transaction and focus on building long-lasting relationships with customers. They're trained to be relational. Because of that, they end up with deep relationships with customers who do business with them over and over again.

The Problem and the Solution

The problem, and the solution, is not in the *salesperson*, but the *sales culture*. I've been in business-to-business sales since 1971, when I was a 21-year-old guy from Alabama selling acoustic and electric guitars, amplifiers, drum sets, and related accessories to retail music merchants in the Southeast US. The company I worked for distributed a few known instrument brands and related instrument accessories like Gibson strings, Fender picks, and Rico Reeds. We also offered our own brand of instruments, such as Alvarez guitars, Crate amplifiers, Knilling violins, violas, and cellos; Apollo drums, and Electra electric guitars.

I will focus on our guitar line because most of my readers are familiar with guitars in general. Like all of our branded products, the Alvarez guitars were good and just as well made as the popular well-established brands firmly entrenched in the market. Unfortunately, our brands were virtually unknown in the US as well as my territory, and competition was fierce. Foreign-made musical instrument products were just beginning to gain traction in the US marketplace. Our products were made in Japan and up against well-established US-made brands like Gibson guitars, C.F. Martin guitars, Guild guitars, and Fender guitars and amps. Yamaha was also making successful inroads in the US during this time. Those brands were established as the "asked-for" brands by consumers who, frankly, didn't know any better. They asked for those brands because their grandfather or father played those legacy brands.

Those landed gentry brands fiercely defended their market share by being very protective of their dealers. Their dealers reciprocated by refusing to sell competitive brands, especially foreign-made brands. Compared to the 21st century e-commerce environment, retail from 1965–2000 was a unique time in the musical instrument products and pro audio industry. Manufacturers were honored to be associated with certain retailers so they could say "X" retailer in "Any town USA" was their chosen retailer and "X" retailer was just as proud to say they were the "exclusive retailer" of that manufacturer in their area. These were not franchises. The business relationship was called limited distribution based on a handshake between the local dealer and the field sales rep. There were very few dealer agreements in those days. If there was a dealer agreement in place, it did not cover territory, demographics, or minimum annual sales commitments. This was the era of win-win partnership, sealed with a handshake, and it was highly revered and honored.

Because of long-standing brand loyalty, we had to find another way to penetrate this protected market of consumers (the end users) and retailers, so I began learning everything I could about how to create awareness and penetrate markets that were seemingly impenetrable.

We couldn't compete on brand recognition, because we were one of the least known brands. We were new to the market. We could compete on value for the dollar, because specification for specification, we were at least equal to and often better than those brands. But value is only important when a retailer takes the time to understand that value and relate it to their customers' needs, which they weren't willing to do. They also needed to be willing to present *solutions* to those customers instead of just responding by selling whatever the customer asked for, even if that brand wasn't the right fit for what their customer needed.

Though it seemed to be a big problem, the more I learned about sales and sales cultures, the more I began to apply several Codes that helped me increase awareness and connect better with my potential customers. These Codes—or *Customer Success Codes* as I call them here—weren't *created by* me, and aren't about me. I just collected these Codes through experience and common sense, and applied them to build deep relationships and never had to worry about sales quotas, chasing purchase orders to make the month, quarter, or year. I curated ideas, concepts, and best practices from successful salespeople who had traveled similar paths before me. I named the Codes as I learned them from experience and hundreds of sources. Together, they're a playbook for how to succeed in sales by developing a customer-success mindset and creating what I feel is the proper sales culture. I believe culture always trumps strategy.

The principles are synthesized into 18 simple but Immutable Codes of Customer Success. I followed the 18 Immutable Codes of Customer Success for more than four decades. These Codes helped me penetrate markets that were seemingly on lockdown. And since I started sharing them with other salespeople more than two decades ago, they have collectively helped thousands of other salespeople build better relationships with their customers, too.

The Instruments Nobody Knew About

The 18 Immutable Codes of Customer Success taught me that before my customer would be receptive to me, I first needed to go deeper in my understanding of what my customer's customers wanted, the musical instruments products industry, and what the people of influence to the end users of my products valued.

To do that, I went straight to the consumers/end users for the products I was selling. In this case, the end users were guitar students and hotel-lounge musicians. To connect with guitar students, I met with music teachers. For hotel-lounge musicians, I'd go straight to hotel lounges as soon as I checked into the hotel for the night. Remember, this was the 1970s and '80s. Most hotels had lounges with local, live music from part-time musicians who played nights for fun and to earn few extra dollars. These musicians still dreamed of going pro, so they made sure they had the best instruments and accessories they could afford. They lived off of their 40-hour day job income and used the money they earned by playing gigs to buy their gear.

The music teachers and hotel-lounge musicians were also local influencers, because they were respected by a number of people for their choices of instruments and accessories. The fact the teachers influenced students' lives gave them credibility with the students' parents (the relevant pocketbook responsible for buying the instruments I was selling). The local hotel band influenced other players as well as local retailers because they regularly purchased accessories and instruments.

That was my in. I needed to learn what was important to music teachers and hotel-lounge players. Once I did that, I could make sales to groups of students, through their teachers, and convince local retailers that they could make more sales and have happier customers if they carried our instruments, assuming our instruments fulfilled the teachers' and hotel-lounge players' needs.

To learn what they needed, I interviewed several teachers and lounge players. In interviewing them, I learned the biggest desire was to have a quality, unique tone and sound for a good price. The instruments must be easy to play, especially for students. This matched what I was selling perfectly, but until someone gave my instruments a chance, they'd never know. I knew exactly what to say, but I needed a way to say it so the instrument retailers would listen.

The 18 Immutable Codes of Customer Success told me I needed to both speak their language and have enough enthusiasm and support from the influencers that I could show the retailers that their business would expand and be better if they carried my products. I needed to change my sales approach and conversations to connect our product to the real needs of the ultimate purchasers and influencers. I also needed to present it to the retailers in a way that let them know that I understood their wants, as well as their customers' wants, and that buying our product could potentially transform their business.

The ultimate purchasers and influencers wanted more than just the lower price that we offered. That was important for us, because our instruments had a unique tone that brought attention to the instrument and helped the musician sound unique and stand out in a good way. I knew that, but I needed the influencers to learn it, too.

With a perfect match between a key feature of our instruments and the desires of the end users and influencers, the 18 Immutable Codes of Customer Success sent me on the road to meet with more influencers and end users. There, I could build the awareness and excitement we needed in order to be able to show my customer that buying from us would be good for them.

To do that, I filled my trunk with samples and visited end users and influencers in the evenings or early mornings. In the evenings, I visited lounges, making sure to get there when the bands were setting up their gear. I'd introduce myself and ask them to tell me about themselves, their band, and their instruments. Then, as now, musicians revered their instruments as fine tools to help them create their art of music.

After we talked for a few minutes, I asked if I could listen to their first set. Naturally, they were happy to have me stick around, and I listened with as much passion as they had for playing their music. I gave them nods and thumbs up between songs. I applauded every song and most of the time was the cheerleader of the audience. After the first set, I thanked them for their music and then asked if they'd be willing to play a new and different instrument on the next set to give me input. Almost 100% said yes and asked me to show them the instrument.

Because I knew they wanted a quality instrument and sound, I made sure to present my instrument to them as an artist unveiling a fine painting, slowly and carefully opening the case and deliberately removing a velvet-type cloth covering the guitar. I didn't just hand them a case. I continued to move slowly, taking great care to protect the instrument and project the appropriate level of quality. Because I invested time and energy to meet with them and listen intently, I built rapport with them. The fact that I worked directly with the factory and treated my product with such pride and care gave me additional credibility and created an additional image of quality for the instrument. At this point, they still had no idea what the guitar cost, but in their mind, it was one to be valued, if for no other reason than how I took care of it. Nobody asked how much it cost. They just played it a little and agreed to use it for their second set.

After the second set, I asked for their input about the instrument. The first thing I asked about was the feel: How did they feel when playing the instrument? This helped me tap into their *feeling brain* so I could close off their *skeptical brain*, which would irrationally stay loyal to the known brand. By doing so, it helped me focus on the features that matched what I knew were most people's real desires in an instrument—quality and sound.

I asked "If you were a guitar maker, what would you do differently?" This made them look at the build quality of the instrument, which I knew was just as good, if not better, than the asked-for brands. Again, this focused their brain on features that mattered to them that our instruments would score well with. It kept their minds away from the brand name. Rarely did they find fault with our quality.

Once we established that the sound and build quality were great, they were *always* surprised to hear the retail price was lower than they thought the instrument would sell for. When I wasn't with musicians at hotel lounges, I visited local guitar user groups to show off our products (Yes, in those days there were user groups for all types of stuff!). I also hosted an early breakfast for guitar teachers to meet and greet each other and learn about new instruments coming into the market, which were the brands I represented. During these conversations, I took the same great care with the instruments and asked the same quality-focused questions to build perceived value and focus the conversation on the qualities I learned were most important.

These presentations and conversations wouldn't have been possible without the 18 Immutable Codes of Customer Success. Not only did those Codes tell me where to look, they told me what to do, how to act, and what to say. That combination created huge perceived value in the minds of the people who mattered most to the retailers who wouldn't listen.

The Retailers Who Wouldn't Listen

After generating buzz with the end users and influencers, and getting permission to drop their name as someone who had played our instruments, the 18 Immutable Codes of Customer Success taught me I was finally ready to call on my target retailer. I was clear that it wasn't an endorsement, just dropping the name of a local influencer to let the retailer know I knew the market and had the pulse of the people who mattered most to the retailers. More times than not, the retailers were receptive to speaking with me.

I kept in touch with local influencers and continued to deepen my relationships with them. To them and the retailers, I became the factory representative who took time to understand what was most important to the ultimate users of the products. I became the one who cared enough to meet with the influencers first and ask them about their experiences instead of harassing buyers from the retailers with canned presentations about features they didn't care about or with a sales pitch that was either all about price or, worse yet, all about me or my products. I was the salesperson who spoke their language and cared more about them than about myself.

I built credibility with my customers (the retailers) because I had built credibility with their influencers (teachers, students, and working musicians). Over time, even if the gentry retailer in an area refused to carry my brand, there was always a new retailer in the area that needed brands to sell. And because the iconic brands refused to speak with new retailers out of loyalty to the gentry retailers, I had an opportunity to help them move from an unknown to known status in their market because I built relationships with the end users and influencers, who loved visiting new retailers in their area to see, touch, and feel new products and find great-sounding products in their budgets. My relationships with them helped the newer retailers connect with the influencers and that, in turn, helped me build deeper relationships with both the influencers and the new retailers. It was a perfect fit for me, my customers, and their customers.

In other words, my willingness to help others make new connections, so they could thrive and prosper allowed *me* to thrive and prosper. What was once seen as an impenetrable market opened up several rewarding opportunities thanks to 18 simple but Immutable Codes of Customer Success. For years, I was awarded the top sales award for Alvarez guitars among my peers and, in perhaps the biggest acknowledgment of the power of the 18 Immutable Codes of Customer Success, the iconic brands that once looked to me as a newcomer who'd never be able to penetrate the market they dominated later tried numerous times to recruit me to their sales teams.

The Lasting and Broad Impact
I've been following the 18 Immutable Codes of Customer Success for over four decades since, and it's served me and my clients well. I've applied this philosophy and these 18 Codes to thrive through wars, recessions, market crashes, bubbles, and bursts. The 18 Immutable Codes of Customer Success are easy to apply and help salespeople create long-lasting impact on their companies and customers.

I didn't achieve my level of success in sales because I was the smartest person in the room. I achieved that level of success because the 18 Immutable Codes of Customer Success helped me often to be the *only* person in the room. In other words, I had very little competition with my customers, and no competition where my best customers were concerned, because I applied the best customer-success principles to everything I did.

The principles helped me avoid being transactional, which is the most common cause of not developing deep relationships with clients and their customers. Because of that, even when other instrument companies were vying for the same shelf space, I was often the only one who could show them how my products filled a need of their customers. Thus, I was often the only one talking to my customers in a way that made my products the obvious choice for them.

Two decades after I curated and began using the 18 Codes of Customer Success, I felt myself being called to do more. Even though these Codes are not my own, but rather just a collection of the best customer-success principles I could find, I knew a lot of salespeople were receiving poor training. That poor training didn't just affect the salespeople. It also affected their customers and the end users because the sales conversations didn't address their needs. In other words, sales conversations with a poorly-trained salesperson often ignore the real wants of the customers and end users, and purchase decisions are made without the relevant considerations. In my case, I was selling instruments that were the combination of quality, uniqueness, and price that the lounge musicians and music teachers desired. If I hadn't applied the 18 Immutable Codes of Customer Success in my work, I would never have been able to make that connection and communicate it to my customers to penetrate what had been a locked market, and the end users and retailers would have continued to suffer.

Because of that, I felt called to help other salespeople apply the 18 Immutable Codes of Customer Success to their work, too, so I began coaching other salespeople on building stronger customer relationships in their industries. Over the past two decades, I've trained territory sales reps, people in middle and senior sales leadership positions with companies from startups to high-profile ventures, and everything in between. I've witnessed the 18 Immutable Codes of Customer Success help new salespeople and extensively experienced salespeople who had been selling *for decades*. I've enjoyed seeing how the Codes help brand-specific and even independent sales reps selling multiple lines. I've watched B2B and B2C salespeople all go from chasing purchase orders and worrying about hitting quotas to building deeper, even Celebrated Relationships with loyal customers.

In all that time, I've found very little difference between how the 18 Immutable Codes of Customer Success applies to businesses across industries and markets. In fact, because these 18 Immutable Codes of Customer Success seem to put virtually all salespeople on the same footing no matter what they're selling, I even eliminate the business-to-business (B2B) and business-to-consumer (B2C) monikers with my clients. It doesn't matter whether you're selling to businesses or consumers, because the 18 Immutable Codes of Customer Success teach you that both of those phrases are fatally flawed. First, *businesses* don't sell anything; people do. Second, you shouldn't sell anything *to* anyone. You should serve them well. What do they want? What do they need? Serve, don't sell. Third, just like the first flaw, neither *businesses* nor the vague term *consumers* buy. People buy.

Because of those flaws, I drop *B2B* and *B2C* in favor of the much more accurate "People Serving People," or PSP. It doesn't matter if you work for a business or your products are directly purchased by the end user or by someone else who works for a business and then sells to the end user; you're a person, the end user and purchaser are people, and the best way to connect your product to their needs is to serve them well. In other words, your influencers and end users are ultimately people who want and need to be served, so stop worrying about B2B or B2C when it comes to how you build deeper relationships with your customers and start applying the 18 Immutable Codes of Customer Success to shift to a PSP model that will serve you, your customers, the end users, and influencers much better.

Deeper Relationships with Your Customers

Salespeople's relationships with their customers generally fall into five categories or relationship types.

The first relationship type is "Tolerated." In a Tolerated relationship, your customer sees you and your product as "necessary" and tolerate doing business with you until they find a better alternative. The only reason you keep doing business with someone who is just Tolerated is because you *need* that product to do business, like internet or cellphone service, get locked in to a long-term contract, or both.

Only one small step beyond Tolerated is "Acknowledged." Basically this is just a noted position, but the customer is giving you permission to serve them. The third level is "Vendor."

Vendors generally sell things that can be purchased anywhere, like bread or products that sell through non exclusive distributors, such as electronics retailers. If you're a Vendor, your products don't set you apart; you're one of many people who sell the same thing. Because of that, you need to work even harder to win a sale over your competition, which often involves cutting your prices or commissions to make a deal at a lower price.

The fourth relationship type is "Partner." A Partner joins forces with their customers to help them be more profitable. Once a customer sees you as a Partner who cares about their success, they often reciprocate. When they feel like you're looking out for their success, they will want you to be successful, too, and start giving value back to you in return. This is a very good relationship, but it only lasts until someone else creates a stronger partnership, or stronger offering. In some cases, Partners can take the relationship for granted. It's a strong relationship, to be sure, and better than being Tolerated, Acknowledged or seen as a Vendor, but it's still somewhat fragile especially if taken for granted.

The pinnacle is a "Celebrated Relationship." This is the relationship every salesperson dreams about. Celebrated Relationships are like long-term marriages or a marriage between two people who *really* care deeply about each other. Celebrated Relationships consist of two people with such deep feelings about each other that the relationship is deeper than the products, services, prices, or other terms of a deal. People in Celebrated Relationships feel true appreciation for the other person and what they're doing. They know and respect the other person's principles, character, and more.

With a Celebrated Relationship, your relationship is so deep and committed that it becomes something both people celebrate and cherish. Every transaction is truly a celebration of your commitment to each other. When they buy from you, they're just as happy for you to make a sale as they are for themselves or their customers to receive it. It's just like a marriage in that the sale is built on a deep relationship with each other. Just like in marriage, the relationship is somewhat spiritual. A sale in a Celebrated Relationship is an expression of your "care" and respect for each other. In each case, you feel a true commitment to each other that you're celebrating through your relationship. The sale isn't a "transaction." It's a natural extension, a celebration of mutual commitment in addition to respect and admiration of each other. As Rabbi Daniel Lappin says, "dollars exchanged are certifications of appreciation."

From Tolerated to Celebrated

By honoring the 18 Immutable Codes of Customer Success, you can go from Tolerated to Celebrated in any industry, because you'll naturally focus on your customer's success instead of your own in what you do, say, and think.

I've observed this happen so many times that I even trademarked the slogan "Customer Success is My Mission; Celebrated Relationship is My Goal™" to remind me and my students of the effect of focusing on our customers' success through applying the 18 Immutable Codes of Customer Success.

Customer Success is My Mission; Celebrated Relationship is My Goal™ is more than just a trademarked slogan, however. It's a deep belief and observation I've made that symbolized my attitude and dedication to helping my customers thrive and prosper through the profit opportunities I offer them by selling them products they can use to serve their clients better. By profit opportunities, I don't just mean how much money they make off their customers' buying my products from them. My mission is to help them achieve a higher total net gain, which means they realize a higher-than-expected value and benefit by doing business with me. I make a real investment in their success.

Although the 18 Immutable Codes of Customer Success are simple to read and apply, they go far deeper than your typical sales training. In fact, they assume you know the basics of sales and don't even deal with prospecting, finding leads, or other Sales 101 topics. While simple, these Codes go far deeper than many other sales trainings because they connect you with the goals and emotions of others so you can achieve Celebrated Relationship status.

The problem with many other sales-training manuals is they teach techniques that make you transactional. That will make you Tolerated at worst and a Partner at best. While you can make a decent living as a Tolerated salesperson, an average living as a Vendor, and a pretty good living as a Partner, you'll work harder, be more stressed, and have much less job security than your peers who form Celebrated Relationships. Once you achieve Celebrated-Relationship status, you'll make much more money, with less stress, and enjoy your work much more, because you and your customers will have much deeper relationships based on true mutual love and respect for each other and not on how much of a discount you can get them this month.

These 18 Immutable Codes of Customer Success will walk you through everything you need to do to go from Tolerated to Celebrated. They help you develop the essential mindset required to build Celebrated Relationships. They help you identify why your customers purchase products and services and what their customers need and want. They help you develop a sales strategy that changes from "selling to" your customer to "selling through" your customer, a simple sales strategy that flips the script to show your customers that you understand them and their customers and have a product or service that serves them. Finally, these Codes help you take the strong relationship you build and deepen it more to become truly celebrated.

They're meant to build off each other, but also work independently of each other, so you can read straight through and apply all the principles to your business or take them one at a time, focusing intently on one code at a time as you go from Tolerated to Celebrated.

By applying the 18 Immutable Codes of Customer Success, you can stop struggling, chasing leads, or worrying about sales quotas. Instead, you can start building relationships that can become Celebrated Relationships that serve you, your customers, and your customers' customers for decades.

Customer Success is The Mission; Celebrated Relationship is The Goal.™

Immutable Customer Success Code No. 1:

The Code of Transformation

Focus on Your Customer and Their Needs Before Yours

"Don't aim for success; the more you aim for it and make it a target, the more you are going to miss it. For success, like happiness, cannot be pursued, it must ensue, and it only does so as the unintended side-effect of one's dedication to a cause greater than oneself or as a by-product of one's surrender to a person other than oneself."
—Victor Frankl, *Man's Search for Meaning*

The first Immutable Code of Customer Success provides that, in order to achieve Celebrated Relationship status with customers, you need to stop focusing on what you need to do for your business and start focusing on what your customers need in their business. In other words, to paraphrase the words of Donald Miller, the founder of StoryBrand, the day you stop losing sleep over your business and start losing sleep over your customers' lives is the day your business will grow.

Every Celebrated Relationship consists of two people who are more concerned with the other person's success than they are with their own. Because of that, each person achieves more success than they would have if they were focused on their own success. Neither person wastes time worrying about quotas, counting purchase orders, or chasing transactions. Instead, they spend time researching what their customers need in order for them to succeed, matching what they sell to those needs, and then communicating that connection to customers and prospects through a *personal value proposition*, or PVP.

Your PVP explains how doing business with you transforms your customers' world. For example, take the salesperson whose product is better quality than competitor products. One way to tell customers and prospects that your product is better than the others would be to say "our product is higher quality than comparable brands." The problem with that is it is focused on you, your product, and other products. On the other hand, a customer focused PVP might say, "You'll have peace of mind knowing our product performs flawlessly for your customers." This statement focuses on the value to your customer of doing business with you. They'll have happier customers and not have to waste as much time or money processing returns. Both statements make the same point, but the second one communicates to your customer that you understand what is valuable to them, and that your product will help them solve that problem.

Customers are more interested in the transformation of their lives from your product or service than they are about the product or service itself. The more you discover what's important to your customer and develop PVPs to communicate how your products or services make their lives easier, the more your customers will begin to see you as someone with whom they can form a Celebrated Relationship.

If you don't, you'll be stressed, tired, and chasing purchase orders. You'll be Tolerated, thought of as a Vendor, or, in rare cases, seen as a Partner. You'll never reach the Celebrated Relationship.

Do you focus on your needs or your customer's needs?
In order to make any worthwhile improvement, you must first find out where you are. To see where your focus currently is, answer these questions. As you'll see, these questions touch on different indicators of where your focus lies. Many salespeople are surprised to find out their focus is more internal than they thought.

- Do you spend more time working *in* your business or *on* your business?
- Do you feel like you're in a *j.o.b.* (which will make you *Just Over Broke*), or building a fulfilling *career*?
- Do you spend more time desperately trying to cross things off your never-ending to-do list, or looking for ways to better serve your customers?
- Do you feel more *stressed or blessed* on Monday mornings?
- When you wake up each morning, do you know what need you fill for your customers?

- Do you find yourself almost obsessed with sales quotas or chasing external *success milestones* like "driving a $100,000 luxury car," "buying a boat and a vacation home," or "having a million-dollar net worth," or do you find yourself setting goals but more concerned with building deeper relationships with people while trusting that your genuine focus on the relationship will bear all the fruits you desire?

If you don't know, take a few minutes to think about the past month and answer these questions in that context.

If you don't know what *real* need you fill for your customers and your answers fall into the first part of the questions because you spend more time working *in* your business, in a *j.o.b.*, or chasing a never-ending to-do list, then your focus is more on *your* needs or external desires than your customers' needs and relationship building. You likely spend most of your days checking your phone, email, and calendar, reacting to other people's demands on your time.

The problem with such an internal focus is you'll be stuck in Tolerated or Vendor status, rarely become a Partner with anyone, and never build a Celebrated Relationship. You'll constantly be chasing external success milestones but never feel successful. Most people end up never *feeling* successful even after they hit the milestones they set, because when they reach a so-called success milestone, they realize it isn't what they thought it would be. The $10,000 watch from the high-end jewelry store doesn't keep time any better than a $50 watch from Walmart, but you'll still be chasing purchase orders. That cup of coffee you get from the drive-through window tastes the same whether you drive up in a new $100,000 car or a 20-year-old sedan with 200,000 miles on the odometer, but you'll have to work longer and harder to make those lease payments. And your vacation home or boat won't be enjoyable if you're constantly checking email or returning phone calls to be able to make the payments or, worse yet, never able to take time to enjoy the purchases. You'll eventually burn out, and you'll be stuck in Tolerated or Vendor status—and your customers won't get much value out of doing business with you, either.

If, on the other hand, your focus is on your customers' needs, you know what your customers *really* want and need. From there, you can make sure doing business with you helps them get closer to those *real* wants and needs. You'll spend more time strategizing, learning about your customers, planning the direction of your business, and refining the way you deliver your PVPs more effectively. You'll be working *on* your business, on a *career* that matters. You'll spend a significant amount of time building deeper relationships with customers. You'll feel wanted, respected by customers, and fulfilled by your work. On Monday mornings, you'll feel excited and blessed, and not depressed and stressed. Better yet, you and your customers will all *feel* successful. You'll have a number of customers all genuinely invested in your success. They'll have a salesperson genuinely invested in their success. When that happens, the tide rises for all boats.

Shift your focus to your customers' needs instead of your own.
Now that you know where your focus is, answer these questions about your top three customers. If you don't know, finding the answers to these questions will help you begin to shift your focus and build deeper, more Celebrated Relationships, because they will help you start to shift your conversations with your customers, as I did selling unknown guitars to retailers.

- Who is the end user for the products?
- Who are the influencers in the industry you sell into?
- Why does the end user use products like yours?
- How will using your product make their life better?
- What are the top three things the end user wants from products like yours?

Immutable Customer Success Code No. 2:

The Code of Vision

Serve through your customers, vs. sell to your customers.

A few years ago, a Russian business executive came to the US to meet with salespeople and other business executives. His hosts wanted to show him a good time and American culture, so they took him to a football game. The crowd was large. The stadium was extravagant. And fans were as passionate as any he had seen before.

After the game, the men walked back to their car together. Eager to hear praises from the Russian businessman, one of the businessmen put his arm around the Russian guy and asked, "So, what did you think?" The man paused and looked down, thinking for a moment. "Well," he said, "I've never seen such first-rate enthusiasm wasted on such a second-rate cause." What went wrong?

The men pulled out all the stops to impress the Russian businessman, but he wasn't impressed. This happens all the time in business when salespeople get caught up in what *they* want, or what they *think* their customers want, instead of what their customers *actually* want and need. In this case, the Russian businessman didn't care about American football. In fact, judging by his statement, the American fans wasted their enthusiasm on a "second-rate cause."

The American businessmen could have been much more successful at establishing rapport with the Russian businessman if they made sure every experience, every conversation, every part of the Russian businessman's experience with them was connected to what the Russian businessman *actually* wanted and needed.

Sometimes we all get enthusiastic about stuff that our customers don't care about and we forget that all people and businesses have customers. If we focus only on the transaction between ourselves and our customers, we end up selling *to* them, instead of serving *through* them. We forget that our products and services should serve our customers at a perceived value greater than their financial commitment to acquire our product or service. To our customers, this makes us sound less knowledgeable about their businesses and more focused on what *we* want than on what *they* want and need.

If we shift our focus to *serving through* our customers, however, we can become much more successful at building Celebrated Relationships. Serving through our customers requires us to focus at all times on the fact that our products or services do much more than connect *us* to *our customers*. Instead, we must remember that our products and services help our customers provide transformative value to *their* customers. Our customers don't want our products or services for themselves. They want our products and services so they can build stronger relationships with the people *they* serve, because all of our customers have their own customers, too.

For example, although the customer buying web design services *needs* a website, they *want* to provide an easy-to-navigate, simple online experience to help their customers make buying decisions more easily. The sales critter (as my mentor author Hank Trisler, called salespeople) who approaches the customer talking about the technical details of how the website will be built won't connect well with their customer. On the other hand, a customer success master who talks about ease of navigation or a smooth, proven checkout process that eliminates abandoned carts, will show their customer they understand what they want.

Similarly, the worship leader buying a sound system for their congregation *needs* audio technology, but they *want* worshippers to clearly hear the message they're delivering to enhance the worship experience and transform the worshippers' lives by way of the message going through the system. I've often told system designers that the intelligent message craves intelligible audio. The sales critter who approaches the worship leader talking about technical details will struggle to connect with the worship leader. The customer success master who talks about how their system will help the worship leader project transparent sound that allows the message to transform the lives of the listener, on the other hand, will establish much greater rapport with their customer.

When talking with current or prospective customers, make sure to have *serve-through* conversations. *Serve-through* conversations go beyond the transaction with your own customer and focus on what your customer truly wants. Ask yourself how your customer can use your product or service to transform the lives of their customers. By doing this, you'll connect with your customer more deeply, and your customer will understand exactly why you and your products or services help them serve *their* customers better. You'll transform the way they think about you, their buying process, and any competitors stuck in *sell to* mode.

Transformed customers are like homing pigeons. No matter how far they go, they always return home. In the sales context, this means your customers may look around at competitive products, but if you're the only one having true *serve-through* conversations with them, they'll always come back. As time goes by, your relationship will grow deeper, and you'll be well on your way to Celebrated Relationship status.

Serving *through* your customers.

Now that you know the subtle but transformational difference between *selling to* and *serving through*, answer these questions about what your customers want. If you don't know, ask some of your closest customers. Like with the Code of Transformation, once you understand the answers to these questions, you'll be able to have *sell-through* conversations with your customers to transform the way they see you, your products, and any competitors stuck in *sell to* mode.

Ask yourself these questions:
- Who is your customer's customer?
- What language does your customer use to promote their products or services to their customers?
- What exactly does your customer want to accomplish with their own customers, using the products or services that you sell to them?
- How could your products or services help them accomplish that as-is?
- Is it possible to modify your product, service, or some other aspect of doing business with you, in a simple way to better connect your product or service with what your customer's customer wants when they buy from your customer?

Immutable Customer Success Code No. 3:

The Code of Competition

Competitors are not enemies; they're people offering different solutions to a mutual customer.

How many times have you viewed your competition as something evil lurking in the weeds like a snake getting ready to bite you, just as you're about to close a sale?

My dad grew up on a farm. One day, when he was a teenager, he was moving things around the barn. When he reached down to move an implement sitting on the ground, he felt a sharp pain between his thumb and forefinger. A venomous snake had been hiding under the implement and latched onto his hand when he reached down to move the implement. The bite hurt and the snake held on for what seemed like a lifetime until my dad shook the snake free. As the snake slithered away rapidly, my dad's first thought in anger was to chase the snake and kill it.

Before he could take a step, my grandfather grabbed him and immediately administered a tourniquet to stop the venom from flowing through my dad's body. My grandfather explained to my dad that chasing after the snake to seek revenge would accelerate the flow of venom through his system and kill him. "Leave the snake alone," he said. "We need to work on you now."

The same principle applies to how we view our competition. Sometimes, sales critters spend so much time worrying about what their competition did or why competitors gain traction with mutual customers, that they never work on themselves. They chase their competition as my dad wanted to chase the snake. Their competitors get sales and the opportunities to deepen their relationships with the mutual customers. The mutual customers get products or services that serve their purposes. But the salespeople who "chased the snakes" just end up hurting themselves because they don't work on themselves.

When a competitor gains traction with a mutual customer, the most common reason is because our communications with the mutual customer were flawed. Usually, this means we either didn't fully communicate the benefits of our product or service or the net gain received by the customer and their customers from doing business with us. Sometimes, it's because the competitor has established a Celebrated Relationship with the mutual customer. In the B2B space, it's common that competitors share mutual customers. Generally, the sales follow the strength of the relationship where a Tolerated salesperson will lose out to a Vendor, who will lose out to a Partner, who will lose out to a salesperson with a Celebrated Relationship.

Thus, as simple as it sounds, the best way to eliminate competition is to develop a relationship so celebrated that there's very little risk they'd consider moving their business to a competitor. Your competition—the other sales critters who sell to your mutual customer—aren't snakes hiding under an implement looking to bite you. They're other people looking to add value to your customer. Instead of shifting your focus away from your customer to what they're doing, continue to focus on serving your client and view your competition's activities as just another piece of information to *guide* you in the process. You might *learn from them*, but sales critters who build Celebrated Relationships never *chase after them and what they're doing* to the detriment of serving your customer.

Every sales critter serving the mutual customer should be of one mind, a mind with customer success as the mission and a Celebrated Relationship as the goal. That mindset, if adopted by everyone, would create incredible value for all sales critters and customers, matching those who pair up best with each other. To get to one mind, we must not talk down or gossip about our competitors to our mutual customers. That would be chasing the snake with your mind, heart, and words, instead of focusing on building your relationship with your mutual customer, and we lose, in the short and long run. I'm reminded of the Scripture verse in 1 Peter 3:8–9 (NKJV), where we're told, "Finally, all of you be of one mind, having compassion for one another; love as brothers, be tenderhearted, be courteous; not returning evil for evil or reviling for reviling, but on the contrary blessing, knowing that you were called to this, that you may inherit a blessing."

Your competitor is just another sales critter with a mutual customer. It doesn't matter how hard or smart you work. It doesn't matter how driven you are. Whoever builds the strongest relationship with your customer will benefit the most. You work harder and smarter to create greater value for your customer and make it easier for your customer to choose you.

As you do so, be careful not to get distracted from applying the 18 Immutable Codes of Customer Success and start chasing snakes in your barn. Keep your mind clean and focused on what matters. Many times, sales critters let their hard work convince them that they're *entitled* to their customer's business. This mindset can lead to viewing competition as evil snakes attempting to poison their efforts to build a relationship with a mutual customer.

Because we work so hard, it's easy to forget that hard work and adding value to customers doesn't entitle us to their business. But our customer's world doesn't revolve around us; it revolves around them and what's good for them, their families, and their customers.

Build a healthy competitive mindset.
In order to build a healthy competitive mindset, you need to hold your competition in high regard and give them respect as they earn it. Like you, they're working to add value to a mutual customer. They're also likely applying some—maybe *all*—of the 18 Immutable Codes of Customer Success to build Celebrated Relationships. Your ability to maintain your focus on your relationship with your customer and use information about competitive products and services as information to help you and not to talk down about your competitors will keep you focused on yourself and help you avoid chasing snakes while the venom kills you.

I am not saying collaborate or share information. I am saying work to keep your mind focused on customer success and the 18 Immutable Codes of Customer Success. Answer these questions to help you find where your focus is and build a healthy competitive mindset.

- Who are your top three competitors?
- What are the three best things about doing business with them (from your customers' perspectives)?
- What are the three best things about doing business with you (from your customers' perspectives)?
- What are your competitors' three biggest competitive weaknesses (from your customers' perspectives)?
- What are your three biggest competitive weaknesses (from your customers' perspectives)?
- How do those strengths and weaknesses match your customers' wants and needs you explored in the questions at the end of Immutable Code Numbers 1 and 2?
- How can you use this information in a positive way to enhance your conversations about doing business with you that do not talk down or gossip about your competition?
- How can you respond to questions from mutual customers about your competition without talking down or gossiping about them?

Immutable Customer Success Code No. 4:

The Code of Knowledge

21st Century technologies allow customers to drown in information while starving for knowledge.

Technology has changed your customers' purchase journeys. Salespeople must understand and adjust to the new ways customers purchase products and services in order to build Celebrated Relationships. Otherwise, they'll be stuck as Tolerated, Tepid or seen as a Vendor, at best.

Decades ago, a salesperson needed to educate their prospects about product features and uses. Not anymore.

Buyers no longer need information *about your product* from you. They can (and do) get that online. Buyers are more educated than ever. Before your first conversation with them, they'll have researched and self-informed about your product, its features, and uses. They also often ask others about your products and those of your competitors. They don't need that information anymore. It's all online.

The amount of information available online is changing the sales process. Salespeople used to only need to be known, liked, and trusted, to make a sale. Today, that's not enough. The new "know, like, and trust" sales mantra has evolved into "attract, connect, and engage."

To be a successful salesperson, you need to know what information your customers have, collect information about your customers and their customer's customer, and engage your customers in a conversation that does three things:
- finds common ground
- positions you as a caring thoughtful leader focused on the customer's internal need to connect
- engages with your customer

If you don't attract, connect, and engage with your customers, your competition will, if they haven't already. This is great news for good salespeople looking to go from Tolerated to Celebrated because it gives you the opportunity to connect and engage with your customers on a deeper level and establish yourself as someone with whom they can build a Celebrated Relationship.

Customers will quickly disregard salespeople who simply repeat all the product information available online; at best they categorize them as Tolerated, Tepid or a Vendor. On the other hand, customers will just as quickly view salespeople who recognize the shift in the market and go into sales conversations and activities looking to connect and engage with the client differently as being different (in a good way).

Shift the conversation.

Because your customers already come into your conversations with information about you, your products, and your competitors and their products, the information you come into the conversation with needs to fall into two categories.

First, you need to know the information available to your customers and whether it's true or false. Unfortunately, most consumers have a hard time figuring out what's true and false online. Additionally, because *anyone* can start a blog or post on social media, it's hard to tell what information is correct, innocently false, opinion, or intentionally inaccurate. Know what's out there, so you can correct it with your clients. False information coupled with natural human emotion causes people to make poor buying decisions. You can make sure your customers don't make poor buying decisions based on false information.

It happens all time. During the 2016 US presidential election, social media was filled with false news about the candidates, created to bring negative attention to candidates (and collect information for advertisers). The articles were mocked up to look like they were from credible sources, causing unsuspecting readers to be drawn in, make assumptions, believe the article (or not), and share the article within their sphere of influence. Candidates had teams of people whose jobs were to correct the false information, because false information spreads fast.

You may not be running for political office, but you need to be aware of the information about you online and be ready to address it. Reviews with false information about products are sometimes posted by competitors as fake reviews or articles. Some reviewers are paid to post negative reviews. It happens, unfortunately. Set a Google alert for your product, company, competitors, and their products so Google emails you all new articles about those topics. Repeatedly review any relevant review sites so you know what's being said about your company, because your customers are looking. Customers *must* have *real* knowledge about your products and services in order for them to get transformative value. Without full and complete knowledge, they'll make poor purchase decisions and buy products or services that don't fit their real needs and don't serve *their* customers as well as they could.

Second, knowledge you bring to your customer needs to focus on the *profit opportunities* your customer will have if they do business with you. In other words, you need to know why doing business with you is their best opportunity to make money.

Learn what your customer's customers want and need. Learn about why your customer's customers purchase. Learn what true and false information exists about your products. Then be prepared to deliver *knowledge* to your customers and prospects that dispel the false information while letting them know why doing business with you is a more profitable decision for them.

That's the knowledge that matters today. *That's* the knowledge that'll transform *their* business. And *that's* the knowledge that'll help you build Celebrated Relationships. Here are six ways to be prepared to be transformational to your customers through the code of knowledge:

1. Recognize that information is just data. Regardless of the source, that data could be accurate or flawed. Know the information available to your customers and prospects about *your* products as well as those of your competition.

2. Talk with—and listen to—your customers about the information. Ask customers and prospects what they know about you or your product. This will tell you *what* information they have. Then ask how they interpret the information. This will give you valuable insights into the minds of your customers and prospects.

3. When your customer or prospect shares what information they know, summarize it back to them to ensure you understand them. Seek clarification if you don't understand them. Once you're both on the same page, then you can move to the transactional portion of the relationship.

4. Recognize the importance of factual data to your customers and prospects. It's your duty to ensure they have the right, true information about doing business with you and how it can transform *their* business.

5. Address false information in a respectful manner to maintain and present credibility. Additionally, the source of the false data could be respected and trusted by the customer or prospect. You can damage your relationship with them by being disrespectful, even if your data is correct. Maintain an attitude as if to say the poster could simply be mistaken and you're there to provide the correct information.

6. Help your customer or prospect use accurate data to transform their business. If they're the only customer who knows the information is inaccurate and why, they can also be the only customer who can provide a better solution to their customers. Help them turn the correct information into knowledge that helps them meet their business needs.

Immutable Customer Success Code No. 5:

The Code of Profits

Customers create profits; salespeople and technology don't.

Profitability is the core of business performance and management. It represents the bottom line for every company. Without profits, you won't be in business for long, but many salespeople don't know the *true* source of profits. The *true* source of profits is a company's ability to help their customers succeed. The more customers you help succeed—and the more successful you help them become—the more profitable you and your company will become.

Thus, to preserve margins and ensure profitability, companies and salespeople need to keep their focus on *customer success* rather than *customer transactions*. Too many companies get this wrong. With the expansion of technology, access to information, and simplicity of connecting with people around the world, margins can become squeezed, while at the same time e-commerce technology and self-service business models disrupt traditional ways of doing business. Order-entry technology is rapidly overtaking the personal-touch model of business.

In the B2B sales channel, companies are eliminating field sales staff, thinking order-entry technology can replace human touch for a fraction of the cost. While that might be the case in the short term, the loss of field staff reduces your ability to build Celebrated Relationships with customers. Essentially, you're designing your company to be stuck in Tolerated, Tepid or Vendor status by removing that personal touch, and your relationship with your customers will only last as long as your competition does't come along with a more efficient technology or a lower price. Your margins will tighten, and your profitability will shrink.

To preserve margins and ensure profitability, companies need to focus their activities on what will help their customers succeed. Customers want and need human connection to help make their final purchase decision. No automated system can correct false information online. No automated system can listen to the customer to help them identify profit opportunities for them. The best salespeople know this and communicate it to their customers as a benefit of doing business with them.

Study after study confirms that after customers research information online, they want a human connection to help them finalize their purchase decision. How many times have you called customer support from a company only to get frustrated having to maneuver through numeric prompts hoping to reach a human? Your customers feel the same way. Technology can be helpful to expedite the transactional side of sales, but the right human interaction is necessary if you want to build Celebrated Relationships.

In April 2016, Forrester Research Group estimated that 1 million US B2B salespeople will lose their jobs to self-service e-commerce by 2020, accounting for 20% of the B2B sales force. While this may be the case, it also provides incredible opportunities for salespeople and leaders who understand that profits come from *customers*, not technology or salespeople. Companies with leaders and salespeople who understand this will have a great opportunity to become stronger, even as the industry reshapes itself. Although I agree traditional *professional visitors* will soon be eliminated, if they haven't already been, there will always be a place for business-development specialists who focus on *selling through* their customers instead of *selling to* their customers. Completely removing human interaction is a surefire way to get stuck *selling to* your customers.

When looking to build your profitability, focus on what you can do to help your customers and prospects make better purchase decisions so they can make more money and provide a better solution to their customers. By doing so, you'll position yourself to build Celebrated Relationships while you increase profits. Although you can automate processes like order entry, this should be done to *facilitate* sales, not thinking it'll *make* any sales over the long term.

To increase both margin and profits over the long term, take care of customer relationships first, work with customers who appreciate your interest in helping them succeed, and automate only to the extent that it frees you up to serve your customers better. With that in place, your customers will become more profitable and do more business with you, making *you* more profitable, and positioning you to solidify a true Celebrated Relationship. This is all possible once you recognize that customers are the source of your profits and your ability to help them become more profitable determines your own level of success

Immutable Customer Success Code No. 6:

The Code of Significance

"Success is what we do for ourselves; significance is what we do for others."—John Maxwell

Behind every great person is a group of people who supported them. No matter how hard they worked, nobody has achieved their greatness alone. Every one of them had people around them who supported their dreams and vision. In order for you to achieve greatness, you must also work hard and smart, while building the right relationships with people who will support you. Until you do, you may find short-term success, but you'll find it impossible to achieve long-term, meaningful significance.

One of the best examples of the power of meaningful relationships regarding achieving significance is the relationship between Jonathan and David, as described in the Old Testament. Jonathan was rightfully the next king of Israel because his father, Saul, was the king at the time. When Jonathan saw David's leadership abilities, however, he knew God was calling on David to be the next leader. Instead of taking the position to which he was entitled by nature of his bloodline, Jonathan declared that David was the rightfully anointed one. He denounced his right to be the king of Israel and announced that he would support David and let David be the king of Israel. Jonathan knew that his purpose was not to be a king taker, but rather a king maker. He discovered his purpose by helping David achieve *his* true purpose.

Jonathan's story reflects the heart of *selling through* versus *selling to*. Jonathan could have ruled Israel by taking the throne and directing people. Instead, he recognized that he could make an even greater impact by empowering David, by helping David serve the people of Israel. By helping David, Jonathan found his purpose in life and achieved far greater significance than he would have if he had focused only on himself.

Johnathan's actions demonstrate the mindset we each need to adopt if we want to build Celebrated Relationships and achieve significance for ourselves, our customers, and their customers. We must all be looking for ways we can put our customers in a greater position to serve their customers well. Like Jonathan discovering he was a king *maker*, rather than a king *taker*, we must see ourselves as sales *makers* instead of sales *takers*. That means we must focus on helping our customers serve their customers so intensely that our customers need to do more and more business with us in order to serve their clients well.

The importance of this code extends far beyond the sales setting. Finding your purpose in life is extremely important and challenging. Over the past few years, I discovered that my greater purpose in life is to come alongside other salespeople and become their *sales maker*, to help and support them in building Celebrated Relationships. Sharing these 18 Immutable Codes of Customer Success is one of the ways I'm doing that, as it allows me to share with as many salespeople as possible the lessons I collected over the decades. By helping salespeople build Celebrated Relationships, I'm able to help their customers make better purchasing decisions so they can serve *their* customers—the end users—better.

By searching for our greater purpose in life, we can position ourselves to achieve something far beyond *success*—we can become truly significant. It doesn't need to be on a scale like Jonathan and David, with the kingdom of Israel benefiting. It can be as small as serving a handful of customers better so they can serve *their* customers better. But to those people, your commitment to achieving your greater purpose is of great significance.

We find ourselves in success, but we lose ourselves in significance. With success, *we* become the focal point of the story. We become the hero. The story is about what "we did." With significance, the story is about the *bigger cause*. We're only incidental to the story, which becomes about the *impact* created. Our purpose becomes bigger than us. When our purpose—or our "why" as it's commonly referred to in business—is bigger than us, we can't *help* but achieve more for ourselves, our customers, and their customers.

Everything changes when we begin to add significance to others. This is one of the foundations of selling through your customers to build Celebrated Relationships. By focusing on helping your customers find success, you'll become much more than a success. You'll become significant

Immutable Customer Success Code No. 7:

The Code of Simplicity

You connect best with your customers by keeping your conversations simple and focused.

"Sounding brilliant is not intelligent; intelligence is making your offer sound simple to understand and buy."
—Donald Miller

The great Henry David Thoreau famously synthesized this code when he implored us to "Simplify, Simplify!" Those were wise words, although, as Ralph Waldo Emerson pointed out, "One 'simplify' would have sufficed." Customers long for simplicity. The human brain craves simplicity.

Keep your conversations simple and you'll keep your customers coming back.

Immutable Customer Success Code No. 8:

The Code of the "4 C's"

Clarity, Competence, Credibility, and Confidence Build Celebrated Relationships.

A foundational quality of Celebrated Relationships is the ability of each party to influence the other. This is because both parties have earned the trust of the other by way of the Code of the "4 *C*'s": Clarity, Competence, Credibility, and Confidence. By following the Code of the 4 *C*'s, they've earned the trust of the other party. With that trust comes influence. That influence leads to Customer Success Mastery, sales leadership, and, ultimately, Celebrated Relationships. As you study your own relationships, you'll find the strongest bonds between people who have consistently high levels of these four foundational elements.

Clarity

Clarity, in this context, relates to the level of *coherence and intelligibility* that our customers have about *our* vision for *their* success. Our best relationships will be with those who are clear that our core values include valuing *their* success over our own.

Our core values are the guiding principles that define who we, our companies, and our brands *really* are. When our core values are clear, the vision for how we add significance to our customers is intelligible and coherent.

We must clearly define what we stand for and make sure our customers can see it. In the words of Dave Anderson, President of LearnToLead, "Ambiguity is the enemy of accountability. If you don't clearly define what you stand for, then you stand for nothing by default." We must stand for something important to our customers. We must be clear.

Competence

We need to be both efficient and capable to build a Celebrated Relationship. Capable with our hands, however, isn't enough. We must be skillful with our hands as well as our *minds* and *hearts* in building businesses with our customers.

When our customers know we're skillful with our hands, they have increased confidence in our *abilities*. When our customers know we're skillful with our hands and our minds, they will have increased confidence in our *abilities* and our *recommendations*. When our customers know we're skillful with our hands, minds, and our hearts, they will have increased confidence in our *abilities*, *recommendations*, and our *motivations*. They will trust us more because we will have earned more trust. We will have demonstrated inward integrity.

Our physical and mental skills are driven by our hearts. No matter how talented or wise we are, what we believe in our hearts—where we store our core values—drives results. Scripture tells us in Psalm 78:72, "So he shepherded them according to the integrity of his heart, and guided them by the skillfulness of his hands." The *integrity of our hearts* shepherds. The *skills of our hands* only implement what our hearts allow us to do.

Similarly, Maxwell Leadership Bible NKJV ties skill and competence to ten keys of Customer Success Mastery or leadership excellence. In the ten keys, Maxwell emphasizes that the best leaders consistently pursue excellence, pay attention to even the smallest details, openly display integrity and sound ethics, genuinely respects others, goes above and beyond what's expected of them, provides consistent, reliable, and rock-solid support, and consistently works on personal growth and adding significance to others. By consistently demonstrating these characteristics, you will demonstrate skills of the hands, heart, and mind. You will be seen as competent.

By demonstrating these ten characteristics, you will demonstrate skills of the hands, heart, and mind. You will be seen as competent.

Credibility

Although competence is important, credibility is even more important if we want to build Celebrated Relationships. We can be the most competent sales critter in the region, but if our character is shallow or flawed, we will never earn credibility. Although we may enter relationships with a perceived level of skill or achievement, we don't enter relationships with any credibility.

We must *earn* credibility through how we act with the customer. It doesn't matter what your sales ranking in your company or industry is, or your job title, or any other accolade; credibility is not a gift someone can bestow upon us. We need to earn it—to win it by consistently demonstrating clarity and competence in our hands, mind, and heart. We must produce for and empower our customers in order for them to consider us credible.

Confidence

Confidence comes after we've developed clarity, competence, and credibility. Rosabeth Moss Kanter, Harvard Business School professor and best-selling author of *Confidence: How Winning and Losing Streaks Begin and End*, said it best in what she coined Kanter's Law: "Everything can look like a failure in the middle." Developing clarity, competence, and credibility takes some time, discipline, and hard work. There isn't a microwave recipe for developing those three integral qualities. There's only a slow-cooker recipe.

Kanter's Law reminds us that the process can be difficult in the middle. Because of that, we can become dismayed or discouraged because we've been working hard and doing all the right things but haven't achieved the results yet. When this happens, I can only recommend you dig deeper, work smarter, and listen to your heart to *keep on keeping on* or *fight the good fight*, as the clichés go. The process works because it works. It takes some time and a lot of hard work. If it didn't, *everyone* would be a Customer Success Master. The ones who succeed are the ones who keep going.

The more you press forward, doing the right things, the more confidence you will develop and the more confident your prospects and customers will be of you. Mutual confidence on top of clarity, competence, and credibility will put you in rare company among the best Customer Success Masters in the world. Both you and your customers will be in a position to influence each other because you will have demonstrated the 4 *C*'s over time and you and your customer will have built a mutual, trusting relationship.

For formula lovers like me, here's a simple 4 *C*'s formula I created to demonstrate the progression of the 4 *C*'s from clarity to Customer Success Mastery, sales leadership, and, ultimately, a business defined by Celebrated Relationships:

Clarity + Competence + Time = Credibility

Credibility + Mutual Confidence = Mutual Earned Influence

Mutual Earned Influence = Customer Success Mastery = Sales Leadership = Celebrated Relationships

Immutable Customer Success Code No. 9:

The Code of Commitment

"Passion is the quickest to develop, and the quickest to fade. Intimacy develops more slowly, and commitment more gradually still."—Robert Sternberg, American Psychologist and Psychometrician

Music changed my life at an early age.

From as early as I can remember, music motivated and inspired me. My first love was the piano. When I was a kid, I desperately wanted to play the piano. I vividly remember riding in the back seat of my dad's red-and-white, two-tone 1956 Chevy Bel-Air playing "air piano" when a song with a piano came on the AM radio. I wanted a piano of my own and, like any eight-year-old kid focused on acquiring a new toy, I didn't stop talking about getting one. Playing the piano was my first passion and only focus, even though I didn't even own a piano.

After talking my parents' ears off for long enough, they bought an old, clunky upright piano for very little money and contracted with Mrs. Moran, the local piano teacher in the Bush Hills neighborhood of Birmingham, Alabama, to teach me for one year to see if I'd stick with it before they would commit to buying me an expensive piano of my own. If I did well in my first year of lessons, Mom and Dad said, they'd buy me a new piano.

That year went by fast and I was just as passionate about the piano at the end as I was at the beginning. Mrs. Moran recommended my parents buy me a new piano and highly recommended they get me a Baldwin Acrosonic piano, which was sold by Phipps Piano Company in downtown Birmingham. In 1957, downtown *any city* was *the* place for businesses, so when Mrs. Moran suggested we go downtown to buy a piano, my parents got a clear sign that I had proven to Mrs. Moran that I was committed to the piano. Mrs. Moran called Mr. Ed Phipps, who owned the piano company, personally to set up an appointment for us the next Saturday afternoon.

I remember that Saturday as if it were just yesterday, as if I were watching an on-demand movie. Mr. Phipps greeted us at the front door. His showroom was full of shiny new pianos. They were everywhere! To a nine-year-old kid, it seemed like there were *thousands* of them. Mr. Phipps was gracious, patient, and kind. He shook my dad's hand, gently bowed to my mom, greeting her as "Mrs. Lansford," and knelt to my level to shake my hand with a firm grip, with the same professionalism and respect he'd treat an adult. As far as I was concerned, he had me sold right then, at the front door; but I wasn't the decision maker.

In the mid to late 1950s, the piano industry was shifting away from tall, upright pianos to shorter, spinet-type pianos. Baldwin was leading the way with the Acrosonic model set Mrs. Moran recommended. The shift was controversial among piano teachers, many of whom felt spinet pianos were inferior to upright pianos. Mr. Phipps walked us around his showroom explaining the technology behind the Baldwin spinet series with detail and how it compared to upright pianos.

I was glued to every word Mr. Phipps said. His presentation resonated with me for reasons beyond my understanding at the time. My dad, however, just shrugged his shoulders and said his favorite phrase when he wasn't interested in a subject: "It's all Greek to me, and I skipped Greek classes in school." My mom was interested, although she was more interested in the furniture styles of the pianos and how they would look in our home.

We explained to Mr. Phipps that the piano was for me, so he invited me to play several of them. They played very smoothly and easily, especially compared to the old upright piano I had been playing at home. The pianos on Mr. Phipps' showroom floor were well tuned. The music flowing from each piano was melodious, again especially compared to my out-of-tune clunker at home.

Cheap, clunky instruments are *the* reason most young students stop learning music in the first three months. Unfortunately, most parents buy their kids cheap, inferior instruments that are difficult to play and so ugly or beat up that kids don't want to play them. I often wonder how much beautiful music never got written because parents bought their kids instruments they couldn't or wouldn't play. It takes a really passionate kid to make it through a year playing on a piano like my first piano. I didn't care. I loved the piano, stuck with it for the whole year, and was even more passionate at the end than I was at the beginning. My reward was in front of me, a sea of beautiful pianos to play with the promise that one would come home with us.

After we all agreed that the Baldwin Acrosonic concept was right for us, the only open question was the furniture style. After all, although it was smaller than a standard upright piano, it was still a big instrument that would sit in the middle of our house. My mom would decide what furniture style we'd get. She looked at early American, French Provincial, and Contemporary styles in walnut, mahogany, cherry, and maple finishes, because they only used the ebony finish for grand pianos at the time. Between not knowing how the subtle differences among the options would look with our other furniture and my dad's reluctance to finalize the purchase that day, she couldn't decide, and we left the store without a new piano.

As my dad drove home, I sat in the back seat thinking about Mr. Phipps' presentation and how much it made me want to play one of those new pianos. I know, it's kind of strange for a nine-year-old boy, but he made me feel special and his presentation made me excited to play a new piano. When we got home, everyone went back to their routines except me. My dad went inside. My mom prepared supper, which was still a thing back then until *dinner* took over, and I sat on the front porch thinking about Mr. Phipps and his awesome showroom.

A few hours later, I heard a loud noise coming up my street. As the noise grew louder, a truck came into view with the words PHIPPS PIANO COMPANY boldly painted on the side. To my delight and surprise, the truck slowed down and pulled right into our driveway. I bolted to the truck. Mr. Phipps sat in the driver's seat smiling from ear to ear and an assistant was sitting next to him. Mr. Phipps jumped out of the truck, knelt to my level, shook my hand like an adult, greeted me, and asked if I would invite him in to see my mom and dad.

When we got inside, Mr. Phipps shook my dad's hand and gently bowed to my mom again. He said he was concerned about her indecision regarding furniture style and felt the best way to determine which style worked best with our furniture was to bring the pianos to our home so we could see for ourselves. He asked permission to unload four pianos and bring them in our house. Naturally, my mom said yes before my dad could breathe. I was super excited.

The first piano Mr. Phipps unloaded had a Contemporary mahogany finish. It was beautiful and blended perfectly with our furniture. With the piano sitting right in our house, Mr. Phipps asked me to play my dad's favorite music. My dad loved to hear me play "The Spinning Wheel Song" from *John Thompson's Piano Method*, which was published by what would become a future customer of mine, Willis Publishing of Cincinnati. When I finished the song, Mr. Phipps and his helper applauded my performance. Mr. Phipps then turned to my dad and asked him to step outside with him to talk in private. Fifteen minutes later, my dad returned with a signed contract and Mr. Phipps wished me a great life as a musician and departed.

From that moment forward, I knew in my heart of hearts I *didn't* want to be a professional musician, but *did* want to be in the business of musical-instrument sales when I grew up so I could bring beautiful music to other people's homes, spreading joy and music like Mr. Phipps did with my family. At just nine years old, I was forever impacted because of the passion Mr. Phipps had for serving our family.

Mr. Phipps was the consummate salesperson, but he did more than sell my parents a piano. He demonstrated the principle I live by: **Customer Success is the Mission; Celebrated Relationship is the Goal**™, long before I'd put it to words and trademark the slogan. He was passionate about serving my family, knew I had earned a piano and my parents were one vision away from consummating a deal with him, and went above and beyond to ensure my mom had everything she needed to make the right furniture decision. He wanted to ensure I would become a successful pianist, with an excellent playing piano. And he wanted to ensure my dad was successful in his buying decision, choosing a piano within our budget that my mom would enjoy showcasing in our home and I would enjoy playing for years to come.

At this point, one might think that all Mr. Phipps wanted was to sell us a piano; however, consider this: He came to our home on a Saturday evening in a truck with an assistant and four different pianos. Of course he wanted to sell my family a piano, but he could have done that with one piano. He could have come to our house, looked at our furniture, and made a suggestion. He could have come with wood samples. He didn't. He came with four full-size pianos, an assistant, and a truck. He came to serve us, not sell us, even though he left with a sale. That's a key distinction.

Mr. Phipps was passionate about the business of music and how excellent instruments helped students grow and learn. That service-first approach led Mr. Phipps and his Phipps Piano Company to develop a Celebrated Relationship with the Lansford family that would last for years. We bought music and musical instruments from him for several years. Lansford Heating and Air Conditioning, my dad's company, served Mr. Phipps' HVAC needs for his business, home, and most of his employees. On October 2, 1965, Mr. Phipps gave me my first job in the music business selling VOX amplifiers and Gretsch drums part-time as a senior in high school. And when I graduated High School in May 1966, Mr. Phipps offered me a full-time sales position, a position that started over five decades of musical-instrument sales for me. Mr. Phipps not only taught me the art of selling by serving and selling through your customers, a concept I now define as ***Customer Success is the Mission; Celebrated Relationship is The Goal*™**, but he gave me my first opportunity to apply the lessons he showed my family in my home that Saturday afternoon.

There's a fine line between commitment and persistence. It's so fine, I struggled with what to name this code between the Code of Commitment and the Code of Persistence. Mr. Phipps was committed to serving us and did it well. He was also persistent, taking note of the buyer's needs, wants, and objections; and working to address those needs and wants while removing the purchasing objections. Ultimately, I chose to name this code the Code of Commitment because it evokes a mindset I could direct toward customer service and selling through whereas the Code of Persistence evokes a sense of actions rather than mindset. Like good sales efforts, having the right mindset and avoiding transaction-centered activities elevates your customer relationships, so I went with the Code of Commitment.

At the end of the day, the difference between commitment and persistence is one of philosophy and perspective. You need to be committed to building Celebrated Relationships, selling through your customers, and serving them well. That commitment requires persistence.

This simple distinction served me well for years. I never finished college and didn't get much better with music than I was when Mr. Phipps left our home that day. But I sold millions of dollars of musical instruments and pro audio gear because I'm passionate about serving my customers just like Mr. Phipps modeled. It can work for you, too. I believe it. I breathe it. And I teach it because it truly is a deep-seated belief that people who are passionate about and committed to why they do what they do will be successful, happy, and fulfilled.

NOTES

Immutable Customer Success Code No. 10:

The Code of the Extra Mile

Personal and business success is enhanced by the amount of our willingness to go the extra mile to serve others.

"There are no traffic jams along the extra mile."— Roger Staubach

Only a small percentage of people go above and beyond what's expected of them in their profession. Because of that, it's not very difficult to stand out. All you need to do is go above and beyond what's expected, to travel the extra mile, as the saying goes.

When you give your clients and prospects more than they expected from you, you'll create an impression on them that lasts long after the transaction ends. You'll be the person who delivered higher quality, performed better, or followed up faster. You'll make them want to do more business with you because they'll start to trust and appreciate you more than they trust and appreciate others. That helps you start building Celebrated Relationships to position yourself as the first person they think of when they need products or services like yours.

The origin of the phrase "going the extra mile" demonstrates the effect going above and beyond can have. Ever wonder where the phrase originated? I had always associated it with its meaning, not its origin, and used it as a reminder to serve my prospects and customers better than they expected. When I learned the origin from Rob Fischer, a pastor and leadership coach who was a guest on my friend Ray Edwards' blog, it really hit home. As you read the origin, consider how you can go the extra mile in your business.

The phrase originates in the first century. At the time, Israel was controlled by Roman occupation forces. When soldiers needed to travel, they often forced the local residents to carry their gear for them. Needless to say, the residents weren't happy with either the occupation or being forced to carry their occupiers' gear. They resented the Romans, and when they were forced to carry the gear, they did as little as they could get away with.

That continued until Jesus of Nazareth urged them, "If anyone forces you to go one mile, go with them two miles" (Matthew 5:41 NIV). As Pastor Fischer explained, by complying with Jesus of Nazareth's urging, you will shift your mindset from inward-focused to external-focused, from *what he is doing to me*, to *how I can do more for him than he demands from me*. The relationship between the Roman occupation forces and the locals was irrelevant to Jesus of Nazareth. In fact, the Scripture makes clear that we are to go the extra mile even when someone *forces* us to go the first one.

Going the extra mile is both a short-term and long-term investment into the future of your business, your customers' businesses, and their customers. My first memory of a sales critter going the extra mile was Mr. Phipps. He went above and beyond what was expected of a piano salesperson to serve my family well. He did much more than what we expected. Had he invited my mother to try several pianos in a showroom, he would have likely sold a piano and been forgotten years later. By going the extra mile, however, he created a lasting impact and became a go-to referral for decades, a mentor to me and—through me—to others, and an example that will live far beyond my earthly life through the words you're reading right now.

When we go the extra mile for our prospects and customers, we build trust, rapport, and a strong foundation for Celebrated Relationship. Fortunately, the extra mile doesn't always require you to bring a half dozen pianos to a prospect's home. It can be as simple as delivering a work product two days sooner than expected. Here are six more ways to go the extra mile for your prospects and customers.

Over deliver: In Publix grocery stores, a regional grocer found all around Florida, when a customer asks an associate where they can find something, the associate answers the question and adds, "Please allow me to take you there" as they walk the customer to the right place. If associates simply answered the question, the customer would have received exactly what they expected. They wouldn't have been disappointed. They would have gone to the aisle, looked around for a few minutes, found their item, and moved on. When the Publix associate over delivers through the simple added act of escorting the customer to the item, however, the customer gets far more than they expected. Under which scenario would you expect more customer loyalty? This is a simple action that most sales critters won't take.

Send handwritten thank-you notes: When I began my career as a B2B sales rep, I carried a shoebox of thank-you cards, envelopes, and stamps in my car. As soon as I returned from a meeting, I wrote a short thank-you note on a card and put it in the mail that day. The next day, when my prospect or customer got the mail, they received a personal, heartfelt handwritten note from me letting them know I appreciated them. The appreciation I received from the receiver was indescribable.

Connect your customers with like-minded people: Sometimes sales critters get so busy they don't take the time to think about their customer or prospect outside of the direct business relationship. We are all seeking ways to grow and improve our business lives. One way to grow and improve is to connect with like-minded people, and one of the best ways to show your customers appreciation is to make a mutually beneficial connection with someone in your network.

If you think of someone, even if you don't know why, check in with them: My mom used to tell me, "When someone comes to your mind for no reason, they are in need of something. Call them." This applies just as well in business as it does in our personal lives. If someone comes to your mind, check in with them. This is not a sales call. It's an opportunity to serve someone who may be in need. Although many times, the call resulted in nothing more than our catching up for a few minutes, I was amazed how many times they had a pressing need I could help them with—but they hadn't made the time to call me, didn't think to ask for help, or maybe they weren't sure they could call me for what they thought was a small or simple issue. Either way, people appreciated my outreach, and it showed in their relationships with me.

Send your customers an article to help them grow their business: If you're a regular reader, this one is easy because it doesn't require any additional work. I do this often. Most evenings while my wife is watching TV or reading a book, I sit in my easy chair surfing business-related and motivational websites looking for tips, tricks, and hacks to help people grow. When something strikes me as useful, I copy the URL and forward it to customers I feel would benefit from it. My customers always appreciate my thinking of them and sharing information with them that could benefit them. Some even engage with me about the article. And unless you're sending an article on a daily basis, the people who aren't interested will delete the email and still consider you someone interested in their future success.

Proactively call at least one customer every day to see if they have any service requirements you can help them with: The sole purpose of this call is to ask how your product is working and if they need help with it. It's not a sales call. It's a call to ensure they're happy with your product and, if not, to collect information to help you remedy the problem as soon as possible. This is a simple idea with huge upside rewards because if they're happy, they talk positively about your product and appreciate your reaching out. If they're unhappy, you were proactive and can help them fix what's broken. Hardly anybody does that. Make this a daily habit and you'll stand out.

S.O.A.R.R.™ *(Serving Others thru Actions & Relationships, Repeatedly)*

Immutable Customer Success Code No. 11:

The Code of Influence

"When people are esteemed, relationships are redeemed."—John C. Maxwell

Everyone in your customer's organization is an influencer. From the person receiving shipments to the person generating the purchase order and everyone in between, your relationship with your organizational clients will only be as strong as your relationship with *all* of the organization's influencers. Acknowledge their value to their employer, serve them well, and thank them for their service every time the opportunity arises. Too many salespeople put all their attention toward the decision makers and ignore everyone else. This is a big mistake and not what customer success is about.

I've worked hundreds of B2B trade shows during my 50-plus-year career. In most trade shows, each attendee wears a badge that gives their name and company along with a colored bar with their relationship to the industry or trade show. This helps attendees quickly identify who they're speaking with when they meet people. Speakers, for example, have their name, company and a bright "Speaker" label on their badge; exhibitors have "Exhibitor" badges, which let people know they have something to sell; buyers have "Buyer" badges; and those who haven't identified themselves or who don't fall into one of the other categories often have "Visitor" badges.

Although this method is helpful for understanding everyone's roles, it sometimes causes salespeople to ignore people with Visitor badges. Several years ago, I met a buyer at a trade show from a prestigious company I wanted to do business with. At the show, I made a follow-up appointment with the buyer for the next week. He gladly accepted and enjoyed our discussion. At the follow-up meeting, however, he was hesitant to engage. His mood was very standoffish and I got the sense he was no longer interested in doing business with us.

After pressing him a bit, he told me his company regularly sends salespeople to trade shows as a perk and learning experience. At the end of the day, the group of salespeople get together to talk about the products they saw. When my company came up, some of his colleagues said the people in my company's booth wouldn't give them any attention because they were wearing "Visitor" badges. They observed "Buyer" badges approaching the booth and being served well, but when the "Visitor" badges approached, they got no attention.

The buyer was offended by the way his team was treated by my team, saying it was an example of our character and customer care. No matter how well he and I got along, the way his coworkers felt treated by representatives of my company threatened to kill a relationship before it started.

Needless to say, my company took this criticism very seriously. We learned many lessons from that show. And although I ultimately succeeded in bringing the customer on board, it took an entire year before the inside influencers would give us the credibility and recognition our product deserved.

Sales critters who understand the Code of Influence know that everyone in your customer's organization has influence over the organization's relationship with you, especially those directly involved with your product. That's why it's important to build relationships with everyone at an organization with whom you interact. Only then can you build true organizational reach.

If you only esteem the purchase-order creator, your relationship with the organization will be only as deep as their relationship with the company. If they leave, you might have to start from the beginning again. If they lose influence, so do you.

This is simply a matter of openly recognizing their value as people and professionals, staying humble, and openly honoring the value they provide. It requires you to treat them like they are *the* influencer, putting their input, concerns, and interests above your own. This is the essence of true organization-wide customer success and sums up the meaning of genuine care and concern. Esteeming *all* influencers in your customer's organization will expand your relationship beyond the influence of one person.

When you develop true organization-wide influence, your relationship is far deeper and can endure key influencers leaving the business. In fact, many times, organization-wide influence can yield additional Celebrated Relationships if key influencers leave the company. If a key influencer leaves and your only relationship is with them, at best you can attempt to earn business from them at their new organization. If you apply the Code of Influence to esteem *all* influencers in an organization, it can often lead to keeping the business with your existing customer and earning additional business from the new company your key influencer joins. The key is to build *true* relationships with *all* influencers, to serve each of them in a way that honors them and the value they provide.

Applying the Code of Influence

Now that you know the organizational reach you can establish by esteeming *all* influencers at an organization, consider how you can honor additional people at your customers' organization the next time you interact with them. Here are three ways to begin applying the Code of Influence:

- Bring a dozen donuts next time you do an onsite visit with a customer. Bring it to the stock room to let the warehouse team members know you appreciate the hard work they do.
- Call a key influencer whom you know to have their calls screened by an assistant. When the assistant answers, just let them know you don't need anything from the influencer and just wanted to let *them* know you appreciate them.
- Next time you're at a customer's business, visit the shipping area and introduce yourself to the people who work there. Observe their work environment. When you get back in the office, send them a gift that will enhance their work life with a handwritten thank-you note for all of their work. Tell them you hope this small gift helps them.

Immutable Customer Success Code No. 12:

The Code of Total Satisfaction

Each new and existing customer provides another opportunity to enhance all of your customers' satisfaction levels.

"We cannot afford to have a single dissatisfied customer."—John H. Patterson, Founder, NCR Corp.

What percentage of your customers would you estimate are completely satisfied with doing business with you? If it's less than 100%, spend some time working through the Code of Total Satisfaction.

We live in a transactional world. From online businesses to field rep sales positions with quotas and funnel reporting, it seems many people are consistently focusing on *targeting* and then *landing* their next client, then moving on to the next and the next. They tout their ability to identify a customer *avatar*, discover their needs and buying tendencies, and then attract them into a *marketing funnel* to guide them through a purchase process.

Personally, I am offended that sellers think of me as an *avatar*, and I bet others feel the same, too. We are humans desiring to interact with other humans (most of the time) and the reason we do business with someone is not because of the qualities of the products they sell, but the quality of the people who sell them and the transformation their products allow us to make in our own lives.

While anecdotal—and often temporary—success stories tell us how someone went from penniless to a millionaire in a matter of months through this method, the truth is the percentage of people who succeed over the long term by doing this is low. Many more people fail trying to work this *tactic* than succeed with it. Statistics and history tells us it's a fool's errand to build a business around chasing new customer transactions.

To the contrary, the most successful people and companies focus incredible amounts of attention on building post transaction loyalty with their customers, and not just collecting transactions from new customers. From loyalty programs, to direct outreach, to offering complementary products and services, the most successful and informed people know new customers can bring great value to an organization, but loyal customers bring far more value for the company—and each of the company's customers.

There are many reasons the most successful companies don't spend all their time chasing new customers for single transactions. First, loyal customers are great sources of information. They tell you what they like and what they don't like. They give you data from *real* customers of yours, not focus groups or theoretical surveys. Second, acquiring new customers is expensive. It's commonly cited that it costs many times more to sell to a new customer than to an existing customer. Additionally, it generally costs five to ten times more to acquire a new customer than retain an existing one. On top of that, repeat customers spend 67% more than new customers on average. This is because you've already established rapport with the existing customers and they know what it's like to do business with you. Third, businesses who rely on chasing new customers often fail to build Celebrated Relationships because they can't invest the time and attention to do so. They're spread too thinly and all of their customers suffer.

Applying the Code of Total Satisfaction

I challenge you to spend time considering how you can shift some of your attention to going deeper with existing customers to build Celebrated Relationships with them. Instead of focusing on serving the *total population*, which puts you in a transaction-chasing mindset, focus on ensuring your customers achieve *total satisfaction*. Go the extra mile and call on customers you know to be less than totally satisfied with you. Ask how you can serve them better. Put serving them better at the top of your professional priority list. Continue to look for new customers, but recognize your best investment for all of your customers is to invest in each of their total satisfaction.

Remember, in order of importance regarding customer satisfaction, you're selling:

- Who you are
- What your product or service is and how it transforms lives
- Everything else

People spend money with trusted sellers based on feelings, not facts. If your customers don't feel satisfied with you, they won't even look at what your product or service is or how it transforms their lives. Very few of us sell products without any competition. If your customers aren't totally satisfied with you, they'll buy competitive products or services from someone they trust. They can make money purchasing from many companies. They don't *need* you for that. They can get a warranty from any company. Again, they don't *need* you for that.

But they can't get total satisfaction just anywhere. Very few sales critters offer *total satisfaction* to their customers. You *can* be one of those sales critters by applying the Code of Total Satisfaction. Do so, and you'll rarely—if ever—have a dissatisfied customer. You may have small bumps or conflicts along the way, but you will build Celebrated Relationships that allow you to easily navigate those small hiccups when your customers feel and know you care about their needs and concerns.

NOTES

Immutable Customer Success Code No. 13:

The Code of Truth

Always present your profit opportunities in truth.

It is easier to remember the truth and facts than lies. If you do not know the answer to a customer's question, determine why the question was asked to gain deeper insight into the needs of the customer. It is better to say, "I do not know the answer to your question, but I will find out for you," rather than lie just to make the deal.

Lying or misquoting the truth thinking you are telling the customer what they want to hear is a proven method of remaining in the Tolerated category with your customer. This is transaction centric versus customer centric and requires a constant hunt for new customers that you haven't lied to yet.

There are mistakes regarding information about a product, which is acceptable because we are human. We can't know everything there is to know about everything we sell. However, it is important we keep up to date on our products and services to ensure we are not imparting faulty information which could be perceived as a lie by customers. On the other hand, lying is knowingly imparting false information to gain a sale. The sale may be gained, but the relationship is tarnished for a long time, if not forever.

I remember receiving a phone call from the CEO of a large customer. Their annual revenue with my company was well into seven figures. The CEO rarely communicated with his vendors outside the C-suite. One of his major competitors dropped the price of our most popular audio mixer substantially, was the reason for his call to me. He wanted to know why his marketing team wasn't aware of a price reduction on a best-selling SKU. Without researching the issue, I told him there wasn't a promo or price-reduction campaign and that the other seller was free to set their own prices, even though it seemed crazy. He was polite and asked me directly, "So, you are telling me your company isn't participating with this seller to sell off their existing inventory?"

Without hesitation, I said, "*No way* that we're involved."

He said, "I find that difficult to accept. Have a nice day."

Frankly, reflecting back on this issue, I came across as a lying, Tolerated sales critter. I researched the best I could after the call to determine what was going on with the pricing because my phone was ringing from other customers making similar inquiry. My "sources" within the company assured me this seller was free to set their own pricing, which is the truth. The other sales managers and I had to grin and bear it so to speak because our company only had an MSRP (manufacturer's suggested retail price) *not* a fixed price. Our authorized dealers were free to set their own pricing to their customers even if it meant their own profit margin erosion. To say we sales leaders and our company lost credibility is a huge understatement.

Approximately one year later, I learned the CEO of my company had overreacted on our inventory levels and negotiated a special price for the aforementioned large seller in exchange for a larger than usual purchase order. He did it in a manner that was hidden from the invoice view in our system. Neither I, nor the other sales managers could see any price differential in the system. Even the account manager wasn't aware of the special pricing. The special pricing consideration was handled as a credit rebate/quick pay when the invoice is paid, which is an Accounts Receivable function, *not* a sales function. Our CEO was dismissed for other impropriety issues, but the damage was done.

My customers lost faith in my credibility because I did not dig deeper or long enough to find the true cause of the issue and make suggestions to resolve it. I had forty years of experience at that time, I should have known something was amiss and should have resolved it on a case by case basis within my authority rather than claiming helplessness. This issue damaged my credibility with several of my customers as well as eroded the perceived value of that particular mixer for two to three years. I had to work doubly hard to re-earn their respect, even though I apologized for my mistake of not finding the root cause and correcting the issue. Even though I did not cast blame toward my leaders, I should have solved the problem sooner and quicker on my own. That was a super valuable lesson. I should have done the following:

- Realized relationships are enhanced by way of dialogues, not monologues. I dominated the conversations because I just knew I was right. No way would my company inflict financial harm on others by making a deal for a single customer.

- Realized a true Customer Success Master monopolizes the listening rather than the talking. I was listening to reply rather than listening to understand. I jumped to defensive mode before customers could complete a sentence, which implied guilt.
- Realized the customer is always the customer. They may not always be right, but they are always the customer. They deserve to have their concerns understood and met if possible.

Immutable Customer Success Code No. 14:

The Code of Focus

Your focus will direct your future.

Your customer relationships will be only as strong as the focus of your customer interactions.

If the focus of your conversations with your customers and prospects are about product features, your relationships will be only as strong as your product's features are compared to competitive products. When your customer believes another company's product to have better features, your relationship will be doomed.

If the focus of your interactions is the deal or discount you can give, your relationship will only be as strong as the deal or as deep as the discount compared to competitive offers. At best, you'll make a few sales until a competitor offers a better deal.

Instead, the focus of your interactions should be on your customers' and prospects' visions, goals, dreams, challenges, and on how you can come alongside them to help them succeed. With that focus, you'll harvest *mutual* success by adding significance in their life in a way that helps them add significance to their customers.

By mastering and maximizing your ability to increase your customers' and prospects' success, and then focusing your actions on adding significance to them, you'll avoid having to chase transactions, defend and consistently compare product features, add costly levels of service, or deeply discount your offerings (a nice way of saying "give your profits away").

When you're perceived as chasing transactions or selling *deals*, you'll smell of desperation and come across as just another salesperson who cares only about yourself. You'll be one of a million, a drop of water in an ocean of Tolerated salespeople.

Sales critters who understand and apply the Code of Focus, on the other hand, partner with their customers to help them increase their sales and deepen relationships with their customers. They help their customers succeed. As your customers succeed, so will you. You'll quickly be seen as a Customer Success Master and go from one *of* a million to one *in* a million. You won't be a drop of water in an ocean, but an ocean in and of yourself with customers excited to spend time with you. You'll go from Tolerated to Celebrated.

Every action we take, every thought we make, every presentation we prepare and give should be founded upon that purpose. Just like every step a runner takes is focused on their vision, their finish line, so should ours be. We add significance to our customers by focusing on how we can help them grow, thrive, prosper, and, ultimately, add significance to their customers.

Here are two ways to shift to a customer success focus from just selling products or hawking deals:

1. We must care about our customers and their needs and concerns for their customers. As the old axiom tells us, people don't care how much we know until they know how much we care. To show our customers you C.A.R.E., requires us to show them proper:

- **C**oncern, competence, credibility
- **A**ttitude, advocacy, attention
- **R**espect, responsibility, relations
- **E**nthusiasm, excitement, exhilaration, effectiveness

2. Place greater value on helping your customer than on your personal success. Your personal success will be a result of the value you place on your customers' success. If you catch yourself mentally connecting your actions with a gain you want to personally receive in the short term, you're still focusing on yourself and you're getting farther from your personal success, not closer.

Immutable Customer Success Code No. 15:

The Code of Character

Our thoughts determine our character and our character directs our relationships.

"Character overshadows money, trust rises above fame."—Napoleon Hill

The depth of your relationships will be determined by the content of your character. No sales tactic, deal, or discount can help a salesperson who is believed to have no character. Although you might catch a purchase order or two before people get to know you, your sales will be short lived and you'll be chasing transactions until you burn out if you don't build a reputation as a person who's likable, knowledgeable, and trustworthy.

If your character is flawed, eventually your relationships and sales will wither. You'll never build Celebrated Relationships.

In Proverbs 23:7, the Lord tells us "For as he thinks in his heart, so is he. Eat and drink! He says to you, but his heart is not with you" (NKJV). In other words, our character, good or bad, is revealed by the thoughts we have in our hearts. If our thoughts are selfish, our character will be flawed. But if our thoughts in our hearts are pure, our character will be pure. No matter what we say, what's in our heart will eventually come forth in our actions, thus revealing our character.

People with the best characters aren't perfect or devoid of poor thoughts or behavior. We're all imperfect, and we all struggle with sin. The people with the best characters surround themselves with high-quality people and content and practice behaviors that bring out the best in them. They build up the best parts of their character and work hard to make their thoughts, words, and deeds reflect the best in them.

In October 2016, I went through a personal health experience that knocked me off my feet and sent me on a whirlwind after routine blood work revealed I had elevated Prostate-Specific Antigen, or PSA, levels, a leading indicator of prostate cancer. My primary care doctor was concerned, so he urged me to see a urologist right away.

When I went to the urologist, I was admittedly not in the best state of mind. I was super concerned that I had cancer, and I was on my way for a prostate exam. After I had been waiting in his office for what seemed like hours, but was likely just minutes, in walked the urologist. He came across as pretty cocky to me, but it could have been a display of confidence from his years of success. He also could have been trying to come across as confident to help me feel that I was in good hands, although it made a far more negative impression.

I didn't care for his bedside manner, attitude, or lack of gentleness during the exam, but that could have been because of my state of mind at the time. I feared being in less control than ever, and the power he had to tell me good or bad news made me feel pretty weak. After he examined me and reviewed the blood work sent by my primary care doctor, he told me to drive 150 miles to his surgical center to get a biopsy from his staff and anesthesiologist. Although I later learned that anesthesiologists aren't typically involved in prostate biopsies, I didn't know that at the time and agreed to make the trip for the procedure.

Unfortunately, at the post-biopsy follow-up visit, the urologist confirmed my fear. I had cancer. The next step, he said, was to determine whether the cancer had spread outside my prostate. This, he said, required a painful and invasive exam of my bladder, an ultrasound of my kidneys, bone scans, and pelvis area scans. It was as expensive as it was uncomfortable. Fortunately, the cancer hadn't spread beyond my prostate.

Because the cancer was contained in my prostate, he recommended I visit another urologist, who was 125 miles away and specialized in proprietary surgical procedure, and he handed me a book about the procedure. This book wasn't a simple informational brochure. It was no calming presentation about a procedure to help my body and mind. It was a slick and very well-produced *marketing book*, with over 100 pages of marketing claims.

I agreed to visit the second urologist about his procedure. Although I was treated professionally in his office, I continued to feel like I was constantly being "sold to," and pushed toward treatment and locations that benefited the urologists and not me. His explanations were ominous and delivered in such a way that I felt I *needed* to undergo *that* surgery by *their* person. It felt clear to me they were more concerned about creating billable transactions than about fostering my wellness. The organization came across as a business in the healthcare industry rather than a healthcare provider in the business of caring for patients and charging for that care. It appeared to me as a surgery company, not a patient-care company.

I was turned off by both the provider and their offices. I felt zero connection and no common ground. I had no desire to engage with either urologist, and it felt obvious from the way the staff interacted with me that they didn't engage with their bosses much, either.

Before making a final decision, I prayerfully decided to get another opinion and decided to contact a radiologist even farther from home, at a full-service cancer center in Tampa, Florida recommended by my daughter, Christie Lansford Waechter. Christie did a tremendous job researching the best option for me and strongly, as only a loving daughter can do, recommended I go this route. From the moment I contacted them, it felt different. They took the initiative to reach out to the first urologist's office for copies of all of my records, scans, and notes, as well as actual biopsy tissues to review. They actually had all data shipped overnight to review before I arrived for my exam.

When I walked in for my appointment, I immediately felt a huge relief and connection. The radiologist instantly came across as caring and genuine and gave me a card with his personal email address and cell phone number. The way they talked with me was different, too. It was clear they were in the business of patient care. Although he could have recommended a much more invasive (and expensive) procedure, they said it wasn't necessary and suggested a noninvasive procedure instead. Even the staff was different, going out of their way to show concern for me and my wife. Also, unlike the other offices, which required proof of insurance before I could move past the waiting room, I was only asked about insurance after I decided to proceed with the recommended procedure.

During one of the most challenging times of my life, I visited two urologists and a radiologist at a full-service cancer center and had markedly different experiences, choosing the one who I felt displayed the highest character and concern for my wife and me. With the urologists pushing me toward surgery, I felt like the thoughts in everyone's hearts were focused on billable transactions and profits. In the radiologist's office at the cancer center, I felt like the thoughts in everyone's hearts were focused on me and, more importantly to me, my wife. They were all competent providers, and I'm sure either procedure would have been effective. But I immediately chose the one I trusted most, the one who displayed the most character. Today, my cancer is gone thanks to prayer, fasting, proper diet, and that caring health care provider and his staff; and I truly feel God directed me to an organization of caring people who focused on their customer (me) and their customer's customer (my family), as opposed to their billable transactions. I was "sold through" and now celebrate my relationship with that cancer center and the wonderful Customer Success Masters who cared for me.

Customer Success Masters understand the importance of their mind in the development of their character. Which display of character would you have chosen to guide you on your path to wellness?

To advance your practice of this Immutable Code, spend some time reflecting upon the following, which are based on seven timeless principles about our minds and hearts outlined by John C. Maxwell in his *Leadership Bible*. As you move forward, surround yourself with quality content and people who are committed to constantly developing into people of greater and greater character:

- Your thoughts determine your character, pure and simple, as stated in Proverbs 21:7.
- Your thoughts can become words without notice at any time, which reveals your true character.
- Do not waste thoughts on those who do not hunger for your thoughts.
- You lead yourself and should learn to master your mind, then your tongue.
- Keep your mind focused on what is true.
- Remain confident with positive thoughts about success. In other words, adopt a mindset of abundance and not scarcity.
- Discipline your mind to remain steadfast in what you know to be the right way to proceed. (In my mind, something was telling me the proprietary surgical procedure wasn't the right way to proceed.)

Immutable Customer Success Code No. 16:

The Code of Attraction

"We do not attract what we want; we attract who we are."—Wayne Dyer

"Nothing sets a person so much out of the devil's reach as humility."—Jonathan Edwards

To attract customers who appreciate and value you, you need to first show them you appreciate and value them, their customers, and others. The best way to do that is to stay humble. No matter how successful you become, there's no way to do it alone. At the very least, you need customers to buy from you to make sales. In reality, many people contribute to your success: your internal support, warehouse and shipping professionals, customer service representatives, leadership, and more. Remember that, appreciate the contributions of others, and openly recognize and acknowledge that you couldn't do what you do alone. Stay humble.

Entry-level salespeople or salespeople who are new to a company sometimes fall into the trap of trying to take too much credit for themselves, downplaying the roles of others out of fear that they will be perceived as a weak link or timid person. This is a big mistake. Being humble is a strength. It doesn't mean you're weak or timid. It just means you have—and project—a modest opinion or estimate of your own importance and openly recognize and appreciate the importance of others. Humility is attractive.

An arrogant, offensive display of superiority, self-importance, or overbearing pride leads to Tolerated relationships or Vendor status at best. So stay humble and remember the contributions and value of others. Park your pride and end any entitlement or arrogance, no matter how hard you work or talented you are. Otherwise, you'll come across as selfish and push quality customers away. A humble salesperson downplays their significance while holding others high. Give credit to others. Make others look good. Recognize other people's contributions. And be patient. It takes great patience and strength to be humble, but it helps you build Celebrated Relationships faster than almost any other personal quality. I've observed this over and over again, without fail, over more than five decades in sales and training others in sales.

Here are five ways to stay humble:
- Remember you are not *superior* to anyone no matter what position you have or what your paycheck looks like. You may have more responsibility. You may have more autonomy. But it takes a team to achieve success, and the person with the highest technical ranking is just as needed as the person with the lowest technical ranking. Make it a habit to recognize all of the people who contribute on a regular basis. Thank those people in front of others. Thank them for just being there. Thank them for taking their chosen path of service to others.
- Apologize the moment you've mistakenly assumed something or had a misunderstanding. Be the first to break the perceived tension. Some people call this being the *bigger person*. I call this staying humble, recognizing that being right or wrong is always a matter of degree and not a matter of absolutes. And apologies are contagious. The vast majority of times, when you apologize, the other person will reciprocate.

- Respect leaders and authority. Leaders are expected to be humble and gracious. Those who are led need to be the same. Similarly, your customers are leaders with authority. At the very least, they lead and have authority over the products and services they purchase for their organization. Everyone has some level of authority, which should be respected.
- Avoid ostentatious consumption. We display our character, competency, and consistency in our actions. What do your actions say about you? Does your consumption send a message that you're humble, levelheaded, and outward focused, or might others see you as someone looking to attract attention to yourself?
- Avoid always getting your way. Those who insist on getting their way are perceived as obnoxious and inflexible, and it creates roadblocks to achieving Celebrated Relationship status. It's okay to compromise your position as long as you don't compromise your values.

Immutable Customer Success Code No. 17:
The Code of Negotiation

In order to be celebrated, recognize that negotiation is both a deal-structuring and marketing activity.

"Let us never negotiate out of fear. But let us never fear to negotiate."—John F. Kennedy

In John Lowry's popular Negotiation Navigation class, he teaches us that what we know about negotiation, psychology, and neuroscience reveals that negotiation can be "mastered" with little effort in order for our success to "grow exponentially."

This is true in both business and personal relationships. Building Celebrated Relationships is the same. While much of what we've learned from the sixteen Immutable Codes to this point focuses on serving our customers well, it's important to emphasize that it doesn't mean building Celebrated Relationships is a negotiation-free zone. We don't give away our profits. We don't agree to *anything* to endear us to our customers. We negotiate, but we do it well, with a servant heart and a goal of building a Celebrated Relationship with our clients.

Negotiations are important checks and balances in Celebrated Relationships. They help ensure both parties are adequately heard at all times. They help each party serve the other party well. And they ensure no party accidentally takes advantage of the other.

The key is *how* you negotiate. Generally speaking, there are two types of negotiators, competitive and cooperative. Competitive negotiators view negotiating as a win-lose proposition. To those people, in order for them to win, the other person needs to lose. In over five decades in sales and training salespeople, I learned those competitive negotiators become stuck as Tolerated Salespeople or Vendors, and rarely achieve Partner or Celebrated Relationship status.

Salespeople who achieve Partner or Celebrated Relationship status are cooperative negotiators with a *win-win-win* mindset. They don't focus on both parties starting at two ends and meeting in the middle somewhere. They also don't roll over and give away the farm because their customer or prospect asked for something. Instead, they remain mindful of the *three* people in a transaction—their customers, their customers' customers, and themselves—and negotiate to reach an agreement where all three parties win. In doing so, they're prepared to compromise their position as long as they don't compromise their integrity, morals, core values, or commitment to customer success.

Additionally, salespeople who achieve Partner or Celebrated Relationship status often treat negotiations as having started long before they make their offers to customers and prospects by developing an understanding of their customers' and their customers' customers' desires (often through application of the other Immutable Codes) before they enter into the arrangement, so they can understand how to make those win-win-win offers.

In my early years of sales management—before I earned sales leadership status—I mistakenly fell into the trap of crafting an offer that would not propose a win-win-win scenario. In an attempt to create an offer to help me move my existing inventory in a particular model category, I designed an offer to incentivize my customers to increase their stocking level commitment of that category. The offer asked my clients to order a specific number of each product in the category in order to receive bonus products for free. After briefly celebrating my creativity to maintain the integrity of our pricing by offering bonus products instead of offering discounts, and getting excited for the accolades my bosses would *surely* send my way, I came to experience one of my bigger flops to date because I approached the promo with a competitive win-lose spirit.

When I approached my customers with the products they needed to buy, I realized some of the required models were also sitting in their inventory. Not one customer bought the required products, and I didn't look very favorable in the eyes of my bosses.

After a round of cooperative negotiation calls with several clients with whom I now recognize I had Celebrated Relationships, I learned they were ready to buy the required *volume* of products in the category I needed, but couldn't all buy the exact product mix I had proposed in the promotion.

That gave me the opportunity to create a win-win-win situation for these B2B customers. My real need was to increase the dollar value of sales in that category in order to burn through the excess inventory, so I made the product mix more flexible, as long as they ordered enough of the category. My customers' real need became increasing inventory of products they were lower on and needed to buy sooner. And *their* customers' real need was to purchase the specific models that would allow them to make beautiful music at a price they could afford.

It worked! The revised win-win-win cooperative promotion was a huge success. We moved most of our overstocked items and helped our customers build beautiful displays of our products for their customers to see. And each customer stocked, displayed, and promoted the models they felt most comfortable with and added other models they hadn't stocked before.

Cooperative, win-win-win negotiations require salespeople to change their mindset from "what do I need?" to "where do my needs, my customers' needs, and my customers' customers' needs intersect?" When you conduct yourself with that mindset, your negotiations will be cooperative and productive and your relationships with them will be enhanced. Your negotiation mindset matters and your ultimate success depends on how you negotiate. Just always remember, it's fine to compromise your position as long as you never compromise your integrity, morals, or core values.

My Ideas For Application of Codes 1-17

Immutable Customer Success Code No. 18:

The Code of Selflessness

A selfless salesperson is a successful salesperson.

One of the best examples of a sell-through salesperson is the late great motivational speaker, Zig Ziglar, who traveled more than 5,000,000 miles in his career, helping more than 250,000 people get more of what they wanted in life. "You will get all you want in life if you help enough other people get what they want," he famously proclaimed. In other words, your personal gain is the result of helping others achieve their personal gain.

In early 1980, I had the privilege of working in one of Mr. Ziglar's affiliated companies. I worked in the same office with Mr. Ziglar and got to watch how he worked. From the Monday-morning prayers to the office devotional meetings and the way he treated everyone he came into contact with, I can attest to the fact that Mr. Ziglar never compromised that core value. He lived and walked his talk.

My friend August Turak, who wrote the *New York Times* best-selling book *Business Secrets of The Trappist Monks*, warns that we naturally have selfish motivations. To be successful in business, he warns, we need to push back against those natural selfish motivations. *"The more successfully we forget our selfish motivations, the more successful we become."* And to those who are concerned that a selfless salesperson is a starving salesperson? In his words, *"Service and selflessness is not about sacrificing growth and profitability for some abstract and elusive 'common good' It's just damn good business."*

This principle comes straight out of Scripture, too. In Philippians 2:3, the Apostle Paul writes, *"Let nothing be done through selfish ambition or conceit, but in lowliness of mind let each esteem others better than himself" (NKJV).*

Speaking about Love and Brotherhood in the Jewish Faith (*JewFAQ.org*) shares a similar message:

The Talmud tells a story of Rabbi Hillel, who lived around the time of Jesus. A pagan came to him saying that he would convert to Judaism if Hillel could teach him the whole of the Torah in the time he could stand on one foot. Rabbi Hillel replied, *"What is hateful to yourself, do not do to your fellow man. That is the whole Torah; the rest is just commentary. Go and study it."* (Talmud Shabbat 31 a). Sounds a lot like Jesus' 'Golden Rule'? But this idea was a fundamental part of Judaism long before Hillel or Jesus. It is a common-sense application of the Torah commandment to love your neighbor as yourself (Lev. 19:18). (*http://www.jewfaq.org/brother.htm*)

Put this common-sense principle into practice right away. Next time you're in a meeting or making a presentation, focus on discerning the other person's needs rather than your own. What is it that they want? What questions are they asking? What are they *not* asking? What's their body language tell you? This one focus, alone, can help you almost instantly shift from having a "sell to" mindset to a "sell-through" mindset. Remember, when you sell through your customer, you're making sure you're helping them add value to their customers, and you'll be viewed as someone who understands and genuinely wants to help them and their business. You'll be on your way to Partner or Celebrated Relationship status. When you "sell to" your customers, you'll be seen as someone who has a quota and is just looking to close sales and you'll be stuck in Tolerated or Vendor status. Constantly ask yourself how you can help your customer meet the needs of *their* customers before you focus on making the sale or your quota.

Here are two more important points to consider when helping others get what they want.

1. Remember, your customers are all people. Treat them like people. Care for them like people. Customers are people who have needs, wants, and feelings just like you and I. People like to connect with people and do business with people they know, like, and trust. This is true all the way up to the highest level of the C-suite.

2. Look for ways to lift others up, to pour into them, and make them know they're important to you. Spend time with them. As Dave Anderson of LearnToLead tells us, *"Learn to be efficient with things but effective with people."* Your sales will flow from having that mindset of valuing the people you interact with over the sales you finalize.

Your Next Step

Take Action and Build Celebrated Relationships

In the preceding eighteen chapters, I shared eighteen principles that can help you build deep, Celebrated Relationships with current and future clients. The underlying theme of the Codes relates to business-to-business-to-consumer sales, or B2B2C sales, in order to help you move from a "sell to" mentality (business-to-business or business-to-consumer) to a "sell-through" mentality where you look beyond your initial customer to *their* customers' wants and needs in order to serve your clients so well that doing business with you will provide them with more *profit opportunities*. This helps you form deeper, Celebrated Relationships with your customers.

The principles aren't limited to B2B2C sales, or even sales at all, however. In fact, these 18 Immutable Customer Success Codes can help you build deeper relationships with everyone you come across at work or even at home, because everything we do involves selling something—a product, service, idea, or influence, in most cases—to someone else. At home, you might be looking to sell your dream for the future to your spouse or vegetables to your young child. At work, you might be selling an idea to your supervisor, your influence to those you lead, or your value to the organization to your boss. You sell from the moment you wake up to the moment you go to sleep. Carrying these 18 Immutable Codes with you can help you sell better in *any* situation.

These principles, which I've organized into the 18 Immutable Customer Success Codes, will do you no good if you leave them sitting on the pages you just read. In order to build Celebrated Relationships with your current and future clients, you need to apply them. You need to take action. In this chapter, I'll prepare you to do just that.

Simply stated, reaching Celebrated Relationship status gives you breathing room to talk to your customers about their needs. That breathing room means you can actually enjoy what you're doing, because there's far less pressure to perform or chase purchase orders. Instead, you'll focus your time on bringing those *profit opportunities* to your customers instead of spending all your time trying to make deals to extract purchase orders.

The truth is, it only takes a few Celebrated Relationships to transform your business and personal life. That's important because not all prospects or customers will be open to developing a Celebrated Relationship with you. That doesn't mean the Immutable Customer Success Codes won't help you sell more effectively to those people. They will. For example, if you take a steward-leader mindset and consistently focus on selling through your customers to deliver them opportunities to profit from *their* clients by doing business with you, then your message will stand out from your competition in a positive way.

What do I mean by steward leadership? Since 2007, I have written a weekly e-zine to subscribers titled *Mentorship Moment*. I have often written that "servant leadership" is foundational to business growth; however, upon further study, I have seen that sometimes a "servant-leader" approach can be too passive, and could have a tendency toward being laissez-faire, and may not always achieve the goal. Sales reps/associates/customers particularly need "guidance" which is a term preferred over "managing."

There is a slight difference between "servant leader" and "steward leader." Both exemplify the character of giving and care for those with whom one works. However, the difference is a steward leader realizes they are accountable to someone else to not only care for, but also maximize the potential of, the resources in their purview. That means a more active role not only in making progress toward business goals, but in particular when it comes to developing people so that they thrive as individuals in pursuit of a team goal. I like the idea of a steward leader being an equipper—one who exemplifies a standard and then encourages and coaches others toward personal growth unique to them to also model that standard to others (professionalism in presentations and customer success, etc. in their personal style vs. cookie-cutter templates). I encourage you to move from servant leader to steward leader as you build Celebrated Relationships.

In my experience, the 80/20 Rule, or Pareto Principle, generally proves true in this context as well. The Pareto Principle says that roughly 80% of your results come from roughly 20% of your efforts. In this context, roughly 20% of your customers or prospects will be interested in building Celebrated Relationships with you. That's a good thing because, in my experience, it's impossible for a sales critter to have true, deep, personal Celebrated Relationships with hundreds of customers at any given time anyhow.

In a recent sales leadership position, my division served 1,200 accounts. True to the Pareto Principle, 300 of those accounts provided 85% of our annual revenue. Although the specific accounts that contributed to the revenue changed from year to year as some accounts grew while others shrunk, every year roughly 80% of our sales came from roughly 20% of our customers. Additionally, about 65 of the top 300 accounts accounted for 80% of the revenue from *those* accounts, and I had true, deep, Celebrated Relationships with ten to twelve of them, which accounted for 80% of the revenue of the 65 top producers. I built these Celebrated Relationships over many years of serving them through different career assignments (a joy of working in the same industry for more than five decades).

Although I worked with my team to support all of our accounts, I was in contact with my ten to twelve Celebrated Relationships on a weekly basis by email, bi-weekly with a phone call, and every 6 weeks with an onsite visit. I couldn't provide deep steward leadership to more than twelve customers, because I wouldn't have the time or attention span to go that deep with more than twelve customers.

When I wasn't working with the twelve, I helped my team develop *their* group of twelve Celebrated Relationships among our customers. I had the honor and pleasure of leading a team of thirty independent field sales professionals, each of whom developed their ten to twelve Celebrated Relationships.

Collectively, that meant our team served over 300 Celebrated Relationships.

The customers who were not in our group of Celebrated Relationships viewed us as Partners at worst. In fact, most of our customers were in these great categories. Of course, there were still a few who weren't, but some folks just can't be pleased. Don't let that discourage you. It happens to everyone. We maintained our integrity and approach with those folks and appreciated their business, but we focused the vast majority of our efforts on customers with whom we already had Celebrated Relationships or Partner status, or whom we believed had that potential. These 18 Immutable Customer Success Codes will help you do the same.

Although the 18 Immutable Customer Success Codes aren't *about* me, I developed them based on more than five decades of sales and sales training. I've applied each of these Codes into my personal and professional life and build many Celebrated Relationships that have endured good times and bad, peace and war, economic expansions and recessions, and everything in between.

If you take one thing away from this book, let it be that you don't need thousands or even hundreds of Celebrated Relationships. You only need a very small number to sustain a long, rewarding career, and by consistently conducting yourself in accordance with the 18 Immutable Codes of Customer Success, with a sell-through, steward-leader mindset, you may not be able to predict *which* customers will establish Celebrated Relationship status with you, but you *will* build Celebrated Relationships while enhancing your relationship with those with whom you don't build Celebrated Relationships.

That's the beautiful thing about the 18 Immutable Customer Success Codes: like a musician performing in front of thousands of people, you don't know exactly whom you'll impact and how, but you know everyone will be impacted if you perform your best.

The musician performs to thousands of people, knowing some will enjoy it in the moment, others will reflect upon it later that night, still others will come back to it in the distant future, while others dislike it. Their music impacts everyone differently, but they know a small percentage will turn into raving fans.

With sales and customer success, your art is the combination of your thoughts, words, and deeds in communicating to your customers that doing business with you gives them profit opportunities with their customers. Some people will connect with that right away. Others will reflect upon it later. Still others will come back some time even later. And some won't be receptive to it at all. You can't control who will react in what way, but if you continue to apply the 18 Immutable Codes of Customer Success, your audience will continue to connect with it in different ways, including wanting to form Celebrated Relationships with you.

The only thing you can control with 100% certainty is what *you* do, and I want to encourage you to abide by these 18 Immutable Codes of Customer Success. Control what you can control. Keith Kent, PhD, said it best in 1968. At only nineteen years of age, while a sophomore at Harvard College, Dr. Kent offered 10 Paradoxical Commandments for high school student-government leaders. These 10 Paradoxical Commandments are just as relevant today as they were that many years ago and summarize the experience you'll have in applying the 18 Immutable Codes of Customer Success, building Partnerships and Celebrated Relationships, and working to minimize the people who see you as Tolerated or a Vendor.

- People are illogical, unreasonable, and self-centered. Love them anyway.
- If you do good, people will accuse you of having selfish ulterior motives. Do good anyway.

- If you are successful, you win false friends and true enemies. Succeed anyway.
- The good you do today will be forgotten tomorrow. Do good anyway.
- Honesty and frankness make you vulnerable. Be honest and frank anyway.
- The biggest men with the biggest ideas can be shot down by the smallest men with the smallest minds. Think big anyway.
- People favor underdogs, but follow only top dogs. Fight for a few underdogs anyway.
- What you spend years building may be destroyed overnight. Build anyway.
- People really need help but may attack you if you do help them. Help people anyway.
- Give the world the best you have, and you'll get kicked in the teeth. Give the world the best you have anyway.

If you substitute *customers* for *people* in the Paradoxical Commandments and live by these principles as you apply the 18 Immutable Customer Success Codes, you'll maximize your Partnerships and Celebrated Relationships and minimize the customers who see you as Tolerated or a Vendor.

Tommy Newberry, in his book *The 4:8 Principles*, shares a similar perspective on success through Scripture. "Based on Philippians 4:8," Newberry suggested, "whatever you give your attention to expands in your experience. If you dwell on your strengths, your blessings, your goals, and all the people who love you, then you will attract even more blessings, even more love, and even more accomplishments. It's a powerful truth. While trials and tribulations are permanent fixtures of this world, our attitudes toward them can help soothe the wounds and bring about solutions while glorifying our heavenly Father in the process."

With customer success, if you focus your attention on the 18 Immutable Customer Success Codes, embracing a sell-through, steward-leader mindset, you will attract more blessings, more love, and more accomplishments. Others refer to this reality as the Law of Attraction. John C. Maxwell calls it the Law of Magnetism. No matter what you call it, the truth is, you attract what you focus on. Focus on the voids in your life, and the voids grow. Focus on your blessings and strengths, and you'll gain more blessings and strengths. Focus on helping your customers succeed, and you'll attract personal success.

Finally, Dan Scott suggests in his excellent book *Let the River Run* that "a book may introduce a reader to a great idea, but it should also connect the reader to someone who has actually applied that idea to everyday life. World-changing ideas are better caught than taught." When I first read those words several years ago, I underlined them and vowed to implement them in my life.

In the past, that meant looking for someone who has applied the great ideas I had learned from books into their life so I could *catch* the lessons from them. Now, it means inviting you to connect with me. Join me in the free Customer Success Academy Facebook group, where I help you as you apply these 18 Immutable Customer Success Codes. If you prefer more individualized attention, contact me at **_Ernie@ernielansford.coach_** and let me know how I may serve you well. I hope and pray this book has added significance to your personal and professional journey.

Made in the USA
Columbia, SC
01 September 2024

40830066R00083